Monsoons
Memories of India

Monsoons
Memories of India

Charlotte J Lawson

ISBN: 1517503027
ISBN 13: 9781517503024
Library of Congress Control Number: 2015916040
CreateSpace Independent Publishing Platform
North Charleston, South Carolina

Dedication

This is dedicated to my grandmother 'Granny T', to parents Liz and Mike who conceived me in a monsoon and delivered me in Mysore; to those who became my substitute parents — too many to mention; to my sisters Jeffer, Penny and Sue who have their own stories to tell.

To my children Ali and Geoff.

Acknowledgements

With thanks to Ashok and Meenu who make these return visits to India possible.

Thanks to Genni Gunn, Margreet Dietz, Charles Demers and those in my writing groups for their feedback, insight and encouragement while writing this book.

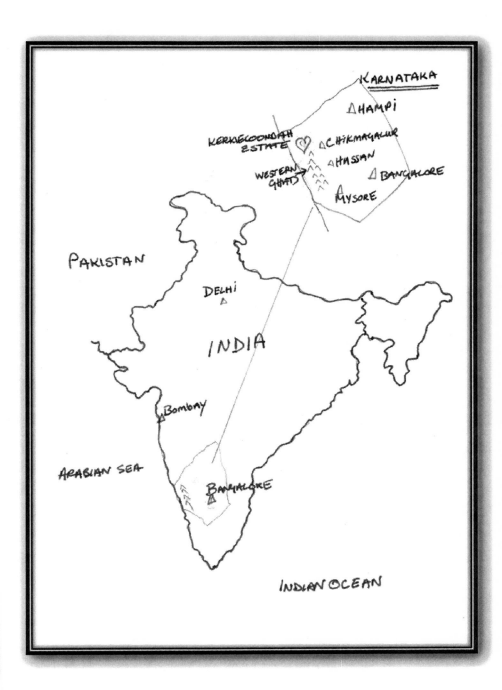

Monsoons
Memories of India

MONSOONS EVOKE AN AWAKENING OF the senses after months of dry heat and scorching sun. The Western Ghats of South India is where Kerkiecoondah Estate is located and the site of a number of these selected memories. The other nearby points of interest are Bangalore, Mysore, Chikmagalur, Hassan, Seringapatam and Hampi. This collection of 12 vignettes draws from a mix of my memories as an exploration of my attachment to the country of my birth, but not of my citizenship. Because India lies in the subtropics and in the northern hemisphere long summer holidays take place in July and August, most of my most poignant memories, but not all, are from the monsoon. Many of the characters are real but some are a compilation of selected memories.

Table of Contents

	Map of India	ix
Chapter 1	Attached to India	1
Chapter 2	Bangles	9
Chapter 3	The Garden of Pleasures	13
Chapter 4	To Market, to Market … Russell Market	19
Chapter 5	Mitlykhan in the Monsoon	24
Chapter 6	Early Morning Ride	31
Chapter 7	Dinner at the Kadur Club	38
Chapter 8	Tippu's Drop	46
Chapter 9	Sightseeing in Seringapatam	49
Chapter 10	Meenu's Biryani	54
Chapter 11	From Home to Hampi	58
Chapter 12	Understanding	66
	Glossary	71
	Bibliography	73
	About the Author	75

Attached to India

IT'S A GIRL! NOT THE son that was expected and wanted but daughter number three. Holdsworth Memorial Hospital, Mysore, South India is where I was born. Perhaps because my mother gave birth to a boy before me, who had died after 48 hours, it gave my parents hope that this birth would also provide a boy. There was disbelief that this baby was another girl. My mother always pointed out that I should have been a boy. They called me Charlotte, which was immediately shortened to Charlie or Sharlie as I passed into my late teens. This was as close they could get to Charles – my father's first name. That's it – no more children. But child number four/five arrived three years later ...another girl.

Like so many children of parents working in the countries of the former British Empire, my childhood was split between India, boarding school and my Granny's house. Consequently I have never truly understood where my home is although I do have this intense pull towards India. These selected stories are little windows into my memories as I explore where home is and where I belong. I have three sisters whom I rarely saw as we were separated by 2-3 years between each of us and kept apart in the same boarding school, only united at Granny's or in the summer holidays with my parents. Yet it is the very mash up of this childhood and the many experiences and opportunities it gave me that I am so thankful for. I carry plenty of saaman (the Hindi word for baggage) both metaphorically and over the years – literally. The sudden death of my father fourteen years ago triggered this reflection on my ties to India. By unpacking this collection of selected memories I want to introduce you to some of the people and places in India who have enriched my life. But first a little history on how I got to be in India.

Since 1746 in the ascendency of the British Empire at least one of my descendants has worked in India to do what was necessary to support king or queen and country and on four occasions died there. For as long as I can remember, the large Gainsborough-like portrait of Jane Harris in a traditional gold leaf frame, hung above the mantle in Granny's living room in Torquay, then on the landing at the top of the stairs, in the cottage near Cambridge, England where my parents retired. Jane was a beautiful woman, fair complexion, soft grey-white layers of curled hair almost as if she were wearing a wig. She sat in a throne-like wooden chair, one hand resting in the other on her lap, and a Kashmiri shawl draped over her shoulders. Her dress was soft blue with ruffled cuffs, probably silk and bolstered with petticoats, like something out of a Jane Austen novel. She wore a smile but it was hard to understand what emotion it revealed. The backdrop was not the English countryside my family lived in. Some speculate it was a fictionalized view of Seringapatam, India. She was my window to the family tree. Jane married Alfred Thomas Keene, my great, great, great, grandfather.

Jane's brother was George Harris, First Lord of Seringapatam and Mysore. The Fort of Seringapatam remains today and is a reminder of the 1799 bloody battle and I know that George Harris was there. Other children from the family, descendants of Jane and Alfred, followed the path to India as lawyers, civil servants and more military men, then some went to the Transvaal, East Africa and Italy before returning home to retirement. Such was the life of families growing up in the days of the British Empire, a vast domain that needed to be administered and protected from the acquisitive maneuvers of the French and other Europeans or the home grown challenges of the Rajas.

By the 1960's much of the Empire had become the Commonwealth and was self-governed. India gained independence in 1947 and Partition had wrought devastation on thousands and left a legacy of hatred between nations. There was no need for battalions of British soldiers and civil servants to remain in India so they were sent home. My parents among them. However, they returned to Mysore, South India as civilians to start a new life on a tea plantation and eventually begin their family.

At the age of five I was left at St. Mary's Convent boarding school in Kotagiri, a mere five hour drive from home, as training for boarding school in England the following year, although I was never privy to that plan. I don't remember much about Kotagiri other than the devastation of watching the black Ambassador car taking my parents away, slowly getting smaller and disappearing down the school driveway. The tall eucalyptus trees along one side of the road gently swayed as if their leaves were waving them goodbye. I stood there crippled with tears. I had not felt this way before. When would I see them again?

The toilet stalls became my refuge from the school bullies. I took my first French classes in this school: je t'aime. No, love was not an emotion associated with this convent school. But later in life I did understand that it was the love of my parents wanting to provide me with the best education and opportunity to go on to university that meant I was sent to boarding schools. With only two of us in the French class, the rest of the children were in the Hindi class. The footpath up the hill behind the school was the short cut into town, through the tea bushes to the dentist where my first extraction took place. The last thing I remember was being driven home because I came down with mumps and measles. I had never been outside in my pajamas, my hair un-brushed, but that was how it happened that day, being too sick to get dressed, I was bundled into the car and we rolled down that driveway and yes the eucalyptus trees were swaying good-bye to me. Once I recovered it was time to head off to England accompanied by my sisters who introduced me to my new boarding school in Torquay, Devon.

Mother wrote letters to me every month while I was in boarding school as they remained in India. She wrote to each of her four daughters individually. Letters that talked about where they had been — fishing on the Bhadra River, how the dogs and any other animals in the menagerie were doing, plus the latest additions of injured animals or birds that had been delivered for her to look after. She reported on visits from friends on neighbouring estates or their most recent trip to Bangalore to stock up on meat and other supplies. And the trip to the ice factory. She included something unique to each of us in her letters:

For me, as a child, it was always the update on Blackie 'my' dog or how many rats had been caught in the pantry this month by the cats. She always closed off with:

"God bless. Lots of Love, Mum and Dad"

Of course father never actually signed the letter but I know he did in spirit. I never understood why she signed off with 'God bless' as she was not the one marching us off to church on Sundays in England. In fact all the time we were children she wasn't even Catholic, although my father was and we were raised as Catholics. Not that Catholics have the only claim on God. Her letters were something to look forward to and arrived monthly, even one during the Easter and Christmas holidays we spent in Torquay with my grandmother.

Christmases between the ages of five and twelve were certainly about presents, the aunts and cousins gathering at Granny's to head off to midnight mass. This was really hard to stay awake for. Kneeling, standing up, sitting down, kneeling head bowed was the opportunity to shut my eyes. More standing, sitting and looking at the intricate carvings around the Alter. Watching everyone walking up for communion; in my mind critiquing peoples' clothes, shoes and fancy mantillas. Time to go home, 1:15 am. Everyone seemed to be happy. It was a holiday so we were supposed to be happy but no one acknowledged how hard it was for a child to "be happy" knowing that her Mum and Dad were far away and not to be seen for another seven months. I became skilled in hiding my true emotions. The importance of Christmas for me was always the telegram:

```
Dear Granny and girls STOP Happy Christmas to all
    STOP All our love STOP Mum and Dad XXXXX
```

Yes, count the 'Xs,' there were five – one for each of us girls and one for Granny. She would open and read the telegram to us then pass it around so we could all touch the words on the pieces of paper tape stuck to the page and feel the love emanating from them. Yes Mum and Dad did love us - me, they just couldn't be here this Christmas…or any other Christmases, birthdays, Easter, or any landmark event in my life or my sisters'. That's just the way it was for colonial families. Our school had many expat families from Africa, Saudi Arabia, the Far East and of course a few from India.

Piles of photograph albums weighed down the bookshelves of the cottage my parents retired to in Meldreth, just outside Cambridge, my mother's family home. The albums were organized in waves of family photos from holidays and other parts of their lives in between when we were all in school. Dad was always taking photographs. His Leica or Nikon were out, snapping photos of insects or coffee plants, which made the cover of Planter Magazine, *the* subscription for coffee planters. He loved to take family photos, which proved to be his way of keeping memories alive and years later I loved to slump into the couch at the cottage in Meldreth, with an album on my lap and let the images refresh my memory of certain events that had already begun to fade. Photos he took and developed himself. Before children, he kept a shikar notebook. This was a journal about their camping trips, including the hunting and fishing details. There would be detailed descriptions of who went, how far they walked before setting up camp, how many days they stayed at each camp, the weather and of course details about the bison, tiger, deer they tracked, the birds and vegetation. Sketches were frequently included and eventually photos.

Mother had beautiful handwriting. Other than letters to us, she was always making lists, tracking expenses in her household budget book and making sure not only us daughters, but also grandmothers and aunts and cousins got a birthday card on the correct date. At Kerkei – the Estate I have strongest memories of, she had a special book to record the number of eggs her beloved chickens laid and had a health record for each of the 25 Rhode Island Reds. She really cared for her chickens - I know she loved us too! Once Dad told me that she cried as if with a broken heart each time she put us on the plane in Bangalore to fly back to school. Did she really? What about you Dad, did you cry too?

Between them they had plenty of material to write a book but perhaps they just wanted to keep those memories as their personal treasure after their 60 years of marriage. They belonged to each other. But who did I belong to? Perhaps I belong in the airport where I can witness and feel the happiness and sorrow of welcomes and farewells. So many flights between London and Bangalore. There is a sense of serenity as you move between

Terminals and Gates, moving with purpose in a sea of strangers. Did I belong to my Granny who having raised three of her own children now found she had four of her son's and two of her daughter's to shepherd during school holidays? Does it matter? We knew we were loved and no harm came to any of us that I know of.

As the years pass I recognize that the identity of my early experiences in India have imprinted strongly on me: on the inside, the geography and culture have been carved to last like the sculptures on the Temples of Belur and Halebide. But from the outside, like the mehndi on the back of the bride's hand, they wash off, eventually.

My father and I shared a passion for adventure and every experience that India presented to us. He showed me the landscapes of Chikmagalur, the rivers where we fished for hours, casting the Mephs #4, three barb hook out across the gently flowing pools. Sometimes the metal spoon would bounce off a rock and glint in the sunlight before the 'plop' into the water. Then the gentle whir of the reel as I wound in the line, hoping for a bite on the way. He walked everywhere and so did I. We silently understood the attraction to the land.

In Meldreth, Mum and Dad had a telephone that worked and we occasionally spoke on the phone. 'Old habits die hard' – they were not accustomed to talking on the phone, didn't use it. As well, the cost of international calling was so expensive so they rarely phoned me while I lived in California or Ontario. When they did call, it was usually my father. The day my mother phoned me I knew something was amiss. It was just before I sat down to breakfast on a workday morning, in Hamilton, Ontario, which had become my home.

"Hello, Sharlie is that you?"

"Yes how nice to hear from you Mum. I'm just about to have my tea and breakfast. How are you?"

"Something unexpected has happened. Dad has died. He……..."

At that point I have no idea what else she said as I completely lost control and howled. I don't think I cried but the pain punched my soul. In that moment of loss I was truly set adrift, my anchor was released. But it has taken me fourteen years to acknowledge that. On the day of this phone call Mum had gone out to the garden to let him know tea was ready. Every day at 4:30 in the afternoon they had tea together. But never again. In a second that ritual was gone. He had a heart attack while tending to his garden.

Through his death I began to wonder where I belonged. Was it to a place or to a person? Perhaps to too many places but somewhere in Mysore for sure. The stories that follow are of the places of my belonging. I was born in Mysore. But I am not Indian. Neither am I English but I do have a British passport and my daughter was born at The Rosie maternity hospital in Cambridge. I also have a Canadian passport but am I truly Canadian? My son was born while I lived in California but I don't have US citizenship – he does. My mother still lives in England, at 95, fighting off every invitation from death, yet I do not feel that England is my home. When I see golden wheat in the field, swaying in the breeze with the mottled light of a slightly cloudy day and small red poppies scattered at the edges, I'm immediately reminded of my parents and the Cambridgeshire countryside. This collection of stories have found their way onto the page as an exploration into why I have such a deep connection to a country where I have not spent a lifetime and where my skin and hair colour shout out: "You are not Indian". My cultural markers declare "You are not English".

When I was eight months pregnant with my first child I knew there was no question that I was going to go to my parents for the birth of my first born, so I returned to Meldreth from California where I was living with my husband. That is what you do, but not in this western culture. But perhaps I am now Canadian. When I drive into the US to visit my son in Seattle the border guard asks me:

"Where are you from?" I reply "I'm from Vancouver".

For now that is the correct answer as I have belongings that keep me here but not family. I have children. Have I passed on to them a restlessness, which they cannot understand? What if my unintended gift to them is an uncertainty about where they belong for we too have lived in many places? At this point in time they know I live in Vancouver and their father does not. I am anchored by my work and chained by my mortgage but continuously search for those feelings of adventure and wilderness my father revealed to me in India. Now I have found that adventure through kayaking, hiking or cycling whenever I can.

My life between birth and 25 was divided between England and India but it is my experiences in India, more than any other life experiences during that time, are the happiest. This is driving my desire to understand attachment to places and people. It is said that "home is where the heart is" but first you have to understand where the heart is.

Bangles

July 1965

Visits to Sringeri were always an afternoon outing. From the tea estate it was about a forty-five, minute drive in the Ambassador. These ubiquitous cars of India had no seat belts, bench seats front and back, and the gear shifter on the column behind the steering wheel. This July we were all home for the holidays — my three sisters and I with our parents.

Once we were on the tarmac government road, barely wide enough for two cars, we seemed to speed along. My parents sat up front and four of us kids all squeezed in the back. The landscape changed as we drove from the tea estate, then coffee plantation, then through jungles and gradually out onto grassland before approaching the bustle of town life. There was a sense of excitement about going to Sringeri, as there would be lots of people there, a small country town with Hindi hit songs bursting out of loud speakers in some stores, while locals went about their business. The bangle man would be there and we would stop to marvel at the selection of sparkling and jingling bangles for sale and Dad would let us buy a few bangles before going into the Temple. At 7 years of age this was exciting.

As the Ambassador pulled into the single-road town we slowed down again. A dog chased alongside the car, barking, but soon gave up. The street ended in front of the temple gates. I was thinking of what bangles I would choose.

"Don't leave anything in the car," Dad warned as we piled out the back seat. A young boy greeted him with a big smile:

"Salam Sir."
"Salam Ravi. How are you?"

"Very good Sir," came along with the requisite side-to-side head weave.

"You want me to watch the car while 'templing'?"

"Yes, here's five rupees and if all is good when we get back I'll top it up."

We walked towards the bangle store. With four young girls in tow, Dad gave us ten minutes to buy five bangles each. Glass ones that really jingle and catch the sunlight, ones with gold paint, metal ones, so many to choose from, ten minutes wasn't enough time. I had to try them on and get them off if I didn't want that one! There is a technique to crunching up your knuckles and squeezing them through the hole. Most English hands are too large for these bangles but fortunately as kids, we still had quite a selection. Not many words passed between the bangle man and us. Although he knew which ones would fit us best, he lets us try out a few by ourselves, then he slid one off the roll for each of us to try.

"Come, come," he waved to me to come closer as he took my hand and helped squeeze my knuckles and slide the bangle onto my arm. One, two, three, red, green, yellow, clink, clink, clink. I had three glass ones, they looked fantastic on my arm just like the local girls. Then two metal ones—I had my quota.

"Thanks Dad. Look, look," I said happily as I shook my arm to make the bangles jingle. I give him a big hug.

We walked back to the Temple gate. I shook my wrist to make the bangles jingle.

"Very good, very good. You need puffed rice? My cousin there is selling for you," offered Ravi, who knew our routine from many previous visits.

Just as we used to buy fish and chips in newspaper in England, here we bought puffed rice in conical shaped newspaper holders, to feed the fish. All of us had our own cone of rice. We were ready. As we crossed the threshold into the Temple grounds, we had to immediately remove our shoes and leave them with Ravi's grandmother who sat in the shade, keeping an eye over a small collection of shoes from other visitors.

"Namaste," she smiled showing her red betel-nut-stained teeth. Her bangles jingled as she moved her hands together. Her sari was swept over her head to provide additional protection from the afternoon sun, a respite from the surprising afternoon sun this monsoon day.

"Namaste," we all greeted her with our hands closed, heads dipped for a moment, each holding our cone of puffed rice close to our body, trying not to spill it before we got to the river.

As we moved across the temple grounds, it seemed we had entered another world. It was calm, quiet. Where were those people who left their shoes behind? It was still hot but heading towards the cool of dusk. We entered the main building and could see at the end of the columned corridor, the top of the steps that went down to the river. The granite floors were cool to the soles of my feet and a gentle breeze seemed to whisper through the darkness to bring respite. The pillars and walls were carved with more than I could understand or appreciate as a child. All I wanted to do was get to the river. This was a peaceful yet exciting place for me, away form the crowds in the town.

As I emerged from the main building to the hundreds of stone steps that led down to the river, I stopped to allow my eyes to adjust to the bright light. There was no one there. I carefully—but as quickly as I could, ran down the steps to the water's edge. With my rice cone firmly in my left hand, I opened up the top with my right hand, scooped up a fist full of puffed rice then tossed it out over the water, upstream from me, as if sowing seeds. The river was flowing very gently so I could see the white puffed rice bobbing on the surface and I waited. Nothing. Another scoop.

Splash, splash, splash. Suddenly there was a writhing mass of grey shiny skin, fins and large mouths opening and closing coming up to feed. Hundreds of huge carp jostled and slapped the water with their tail fins for their share of rice.

"Dad, Dad, look, the fish are here," I said.

The sudden appearance of the huge fish at my feet and some almost on the steps, was always a thrill. It being a holy place, we couldn't scream with excitement, but our faces were alive with amazement. As quickly as they arrived, they disappeared. One of the monks from the Temple, robed in white cotton, came over to share our joy. And to let us know that when the fish leave so quickly it means that there is a crocodile nearby so we should back up a few steps, just in case they come out of the water. Most of the time they are just passing on their way downstream and across to the sand bank on the other side.

We backed up and sat on the steps and sure enough, there was the crocodile, just mid stream and gliding downriver to the other side. The monk leaned towards me and pointed.

"See," he whispered and pointed to the dark shadow in the middle of the river.

I was thrilled and briefly looked up at the monk as I saw what he saw: the crocodile, cruising by below the surface of the water.

"Dad, did you see it?" I asked as my heart was thumping

"Yes it was a big one—bigger than I've ever seen before."

After it passed, the fish returned and so did we, to toss out the rest of the rice.

The sun was setting as we slowly walked back up the steps, through the Temple, to collect our shoes. Another great trip to Sringeri was coming to an end. I thought these trips would go on forever, but of course they did not.

The Garden of Pleasures

BASKARAN PROUDLY WALKS TOWARDS THE lawn wearing his especially white and tightly folded turban and service uniform. He carries a tray with the kedgeree and warm plates from the kitchen. Baskaran has been working for my parents for ten years. Today my mother and I are eating our lunch in this subtropical garden, like having a picnic. Baskaran bakes the most delicious white bread and buns with a crunchy crust and warm on the inside, just out of the oven. He usually bakes on Tuesdays. He cooks many curry dishes which my mother and I love but to satisfy the culinary needs of my father, he has also perfected stews, meat pies and roast mutton and roast beef along with the roast potatoes. His eldest daughter Shilpa, was our aya when my sisters and I were with my parents, and his vagrant son -- who vanished for months then reappeared -- always brought trouble back with him. They all lived in the servants' quarters about 20 minutes walk from our bungalow. Baskaran knows us well. I should have been in boarding school at this time of year, with my sisters, but due to asthma attacks I was sent home. This means I get to have my 8th birthday at home with my parents. The last birthday I enjoyed at home was my 4th birthday – not that I could remember that.

At the base of the tree I spread a large colourful dhurrie on the grass and tossed down two cushions, one for mother to make it softer for her back when she leans against the rock, and the other for me to sit on. Mother unpacks the tray with napkins, cutlery, and a jug of cold sweet-lime juice and glasses. Draped over the top of the jug is a round cotton mesh screen with glass beads sewn into the edge to ensure it won't blow away and allow insects to drop in for a taste of this slightly sweetened fresh drink. It is 1 o'clock in the afternoon on this February day, the same time that lunch is served every day of the week. But today we are eating in the garden, amidst red cannas, pink bougenvelliea, orange marigolds and the lush greens of a sub tropical garden. Lunch on the lawn only happens when father is not at home. Today we are enjoying the treat of our favourite meal, in their most treasured location, on this most wonderful day.

"Is that everything Madam? I will return when you have finished," says Baskaran

"Yes, thank you Baskaran, everything looks very good," Mum replies.

The kedgeree is served in a china vegetable dish covered with a lid and wrapped in a clean cotton tea towel tied first by two opposite corners then by the other two corners, nice and snug to keep the warmth inside. I loved to 'unwrap' the kedgeree, take off the lid and see the bright yellow saffron rice and smell the subtle aroma of all that goes into kedgeree. It is always a happy association. Perhaps it is the unusually bright colour for rice, normally being white, combined with it tasting good and associated with close times with my mother, when I have the full attention of my mother. I'm not sharing Mum with anyone. Kedgeree is a comfort food for me.

It is so much fun to have a hot meal sitting on the lawn in the garden – a fancy picnic. So much more fun than being seated at the very formal glass topped dinning room table with mother at one end, father at the other and me somewhere in the middle on her mother's right. Mealtimes are notoriously serious and silent except when my sisters are present. Particularly at breakfast when one of us crunches toast loudly. The offender receives a nod from mother to tone it down. She will get the glare of death from father that this crunching must stop. My crunching is deliberately loud. Outside on the other hand anything goes.

"Let me open up the kedgeree and I'll serve you Mum," I said as I perch on my knees and carefully unwrap the kedgeree, feeling the warmth of the dish through the tea towels.

One, two, three I count aloud the serving spoonsful as I tip each one onto the plate for mother.

"Yes, I'd like another piece of egg and what about my sardines, you've only given me two! And some crispy onions please!"

"There Mum. Mmmmm". I'm happy to oblige.

Then I serve myself. I love the crispy onions as well, and carefully select a spoonful with lots of cashew nuts, some hard-boiled eggs and a few sultanas. Sardines aren't my favourite food, but I will eat almost anything on days like this. The soft yellow of saffron rice and not having to share my mother with any of my sisters or father, just makes this the happiest meal for me. Mother took the net covering off the jug and pours sweet lime for both of us. As she returns the net cover, the glass beads clink against the jug. She leans against the rock by the tree, legs extended in front of her and crossed, and I sit cross-legged.

"Cheers Mum," I say as I raise my glass, giggling and pretending to be like my parents when they raise their glasses of gin and whiskey in the evenings.

"Are we going to the river on Sunday? I really like being on the beach there. Will you come swimming with me through the rapids like last time? Do you remember that Mum? It was so much fun even though I was a tiny bit scared," I asked.

Mother laughed remembering the event.

"Yes and we were making such a noise Dad got quite annoyed with us. He said we'd scare all the fish away!"

After lunch was over and all the dishes were cleared, we lay down on the dhurrie for a snooze in the shade. Lying next to each other, I look up at the clear blue sky through the leaves, a gentle breeze swept over us. I don't want to sleep at all, but do want to lie next to my mother, to feel those moments of love and safety. Everything is quiet. It is the time of day when everyone took a ziz from the heat of the day and the usual sounds of work on a tea estate fall silent. I knew at half past two in the afternoon this would change. There were things to be done after 2:30 pm. Preparation for the next day as father was away again on Estate rounds so he would need lunch prepared. The chickens need to be let out for the afternoon and checked to ensure they were all accounted for and healthy. And who knows what else, but Mum always seemed to have so many things to do she couldn't spend time with me. As a result, and to feed my curiosity I tended to wander off to entertain myself, sometimes seeing things not intended for my eyes. Even more confusing, I didn't always understand what I saw.

Amazingly, without an alarm clock Mum woke up at half past two. She sat up and announced she must get on with her work.

"Charlie love, give me a hand by carrying the cushions on to the verandah, please".

Mum folded the dhurrie to carry inside and I could barely see where I was going with my arms around the cushions pressed against my stomach and chest, holding onto them. I dropped them on the cane chair on the verandah. Once inside the bungalow Mum disappeared down the long dark corridor that had an indoor swing, to the kitchen at the back.

The bungalow was situated amidst green lawns, bougenvelliea hedges, a tall Norwegian pine tree, silver oaks and a terraced garden. There was a large swing on the second level and below that the vegetable garden. My father had laid down the law about going to the lower garden:

"Do not go to the swing unless your Mum or I are with you". I had always abided by that rule, fully understanding that the back of a hairbrush could be quite painful.

"Hmm, I think I'll go down to the swing for a while" I thought, Dad wasn't here, Mum was busy doing something else. I was ready to explore and headed through the carport, along the driveway and across the grass to the swing on the lower level of the garden. The swing had a wide wooden seat. I had to stand on my tiptoes, jump and pull myself up using the chains attached to the seat just to get onto the swing. When I pumped my legs, I could get the swing go high enough to see over the hedge and down into the vegetable garden. On the first high pass I noticed two people in the vegetable garden, I wasn't expecting to see anyone there I couldn't really see who they were. I pumped my legs and body forward and backward, to get more height and just at the apex of the swing leant forward to look. Who was there and what where they doing? Usually all the gardening was done in the cool of the early morning. I took three more swings and identified who was there, but was confused because these two people were not usually associated with each other, in my mind. To confirm what I was seeing, I slowed down the swing, hopped off and hurried over to the hedge where

I peer through and see more clearly, but without being seen. Yes it was one of the office clerks and Sushila, Baskaran's daughter. She was lying down, and he was sitting on top of her, but she seemed not to mind. They were not talking, but making some weird noises. I had not seen this before so it was a little puzzling to me, but I also seemed to know that because this was happening is such a secluded place and between two people that were not normally together, AND because I shouldn't have been here in the first place, this was probably going to have to be a big secret. Sure enough when they stood up and padded down their clothes to dust off the dirt, they hurried to the vegetable garden gate, where the boy left first then a few minutes later Shushila. But not before she had also helped herself to two brinjals from the garden.

This whole episode raised questions for me, which I could never discuss with mother, because it would mean I would have to admit to having gone down to the swing on my own. I didn't want to experience the anger of my father. I had seen him angry, and didn't want to give him reason to be so with me. I would relive the scene in my memory, again and again. Whenever I saw either of these two people I observed their every move, facial expression, interaction, trying to piece together the full story without asking questions. I did consider telling mother about the brinjals being stolen, but soon realized that wouldn't work either, as I'd have to explain why I was there, so better not say anything. I was just going to have to keep this my secret. But you know how secrets are, they are difficult to hold onto, eventually they tumble out.

In the garden of pleasures

To Market, to Market ...
Russell Market

JUNE 1967

RUSSELL MARKET WAS BUILT IN the 1920's. A high-ceilinged brick building, white washed on the exterior, like an aircraft hangar on the interior, filled with rows of vendors who sold not just fruit and vegetables but flowers, ribbons, bangles, spices, incense and statuettes. Our trips to Bangalore were never complete without a visit to Russell Market to pick up vegetables and meat to last for about three months as that would be the next time we would return to Bangalore from the coffee estate. The head office of the company my father worked for was here, as well as the international airport, where my parents came to meet us children off the plane for the beginning of holidays and sadly where we returned when it was time to go back to school in England. In Bangalore the West End Hotel became a home away from home. The market trip was always done early on the day we drove back to the estate.

At five in the morning we received our wakeup call. I reluctantly dragged myself out of bed as I didn't really want to go, but I knew that if I didn't, mother would be going alone. And there was something about that made me feel sorry for her. Did I want to lie in and feel guilty because I didn't go with her? No, it was easier to get up and help. My father never went to Market, mother did not drive and at 9, I wasn't driving either, so Jeremy, our driver, drove us. The first stop was the ice factory to load blocks of ice into the metal ice box which would house the meat on the 8-hour journey back to the Estate. To get the best choice of vegetables you had to be at the market by 6 am.

"Salaam Madam. It has been many weeks since you came," greeted Mary. She wore a cotton sari, bare feet, and had a coracle-shaped basket under one arm. Mary, who was as entrepreneurial as any of the vendors in the market, always recognized my mother and immediately came to help shop. With a constant flow of ex pats in town she had become an indispensible part of their lives when it came to surviving the market. She knew all the vendors and where the best prices for the best vegetables would be and as she knew my mother's preferences she knew who to buy from. Between them they had a strategy before entering the building.

"Good morning Mary. Nice to see you today. Let's look at my list and decide where we'll go first. Are the vegetables good right now?" Mum asked. "I know it has been a very dry season." Conversations were not complicated as Mary spoke a limited amount of English and Mother even less Kannada and no Hindi.

"Yes Madam. There are some very good vegetables. Come, I will show you," said Mary eager to get us into the market, supplied, back to the car and on to her next loyal customer. She would always receive a generous tip for her services.

"Stay close to me, Charlie. After this we'll go across to the meat market," said mother.

I'm capable of taking care of myself, I moaned in my mind, but did as she asked.

There was no meat in this building as this market was the domain of the Brahmins. It was dark despite having electricity. Each vendor had a naked, dusty light blub hanging down over the neatly displayed goods but not all bulbs gave light. The windows were covered to keep the heat out. The alleyways between the stalls were narrow and seemed darker closer to foot level, but clean because they were wet and had just been hosed down. It was always clean at floor level in the early morning.

Immediately upon entering the building I noticed the vendors looking towards us and waving to beckon us to their stall, promoting their 'best' tomatoes, brinjals, cabbage or okra. The old-timers knew that Mary had her own itinerary for this sweep through the market. At this time of the day it was relatively uncluttered but by about 10 am this was a bustling, claustrophobic and sweaty place to be. As we strolled through the aisles of neatly displayed vegetables and fruits there was an increasing population of fruit flies congregating at certain stalls. Mum and I ambled past flower stalls where the cool morning air was laced with the sweet fragrance of jasmine garlands, fresh cut marigolds, canna lilies and roses. Mother was always up for haggling if she thought the asking price was significantly more extravagant than last time. Acutely aware that the colour of our skin automatically raised the price, she knew when that skin tax was extravagant. The vendor also knew that she would haggle before settling on a price. Mary carried the purchases and mother jotted down the prices in the special note book.

"Price is higher because drought. This is June and there is still no sign of rain. Farmers must buy water – this is expensive. Next time price will be less," said Mary as she interpreted what the vendor said.

Once the shopping was complete, Mary walked back to the car with us, carrying the basket of fruit and vegetables on her head and the surplus in cloth bags. These were stowed in the boot of the car and mother and I headed off to the meat market on the other side of the big square. My mother and I were alone on this part of the shopping as Mary did not go onto the meat market, probably for the same reasons as Jeremy, he was Hindu, so she would not offend him by asking him to accompany us into this carnivorous cavern. It was a completely male dominated environment.

"Here Charlie, can you carry these bags for me. When they are filled I'll need you to help me carry them back to the car too. I hope you're feeling strong this morning," Mum said as she briskly walked across the square to the meat market. I followed, a few paces behind her, looking up at the sky, seeing the vultures circling.

The butchers of Russell Market were housed in a tall building with a narrow aisle, stalls on both sides. Fewer people were here. This was the domain of Muslims. They wore white skullcaps, and dark blue aprons tied at the back, with varying degrees of blood smeared on the front. Each stall had a high butcher's block which customers would look up towards as the meat was cut. Carcasses of cattle, goats and camel hung from large metal hooks. No pigs here. You could hear the sound of metal crashing through bone as the heavy meat clever hammered down onto the leg of mutton. While most of the butchering was done with really sharp knives through the cartilage between joints, some cuts required the strength and weight of a cleaver. There was always a stall that had cows heads – four or five in a row - on the blocks with the tongue hanging out. I though it odd to see these expressionless heads with no body behind them, as you usually do when they are wandering around the streets. Then there were the large round baskets with chickens inside perhaps unaware of their impending fate. In one basket a rooster had successfully poked his head up through a hole in the basket lid, turning his head to the left then to the right, blinking as if deciding on what information to relay back to his fellow habitants in the basket below. There were no clucking noises but an eerie silence, almost as if they knew. The camel carcasses were hung and sections chalked off as they were sold, but each carcass would not be butchered until the whole was bought. The smell of raw meat was very distinct, the flies ever present and you had to watch where you put your feet lest you track blood or scraps of meat back to the car on your shoes.

Mum knew where she was going, but I was too fascinated and a little frightened, by what I was seeing, to notice that her order was filled and she was ready to leave. Once we had the legs of mutton, stewing beef, plucked and gutted chickens and the complimentary bag of bones to boil up for the dogs, shopping was done. No steaks on this list because all the meat would have to be thoroughly cooked before eaten and my father never ate a steak that wasn't weeping blood. I was assigned bags to carry. Back at the car Jeremy had seen us leaving the butchers and had opened up the boot and ice box ready for us to push it all in, then back to the West End Hotel to complete packing the car ready for our departure by 10 am. The hotel garden was a sub-tropical delight with a huge banyan tree, lush green ferns, colourful flowers and a swimming pool, which could be seen easily from the long cool verandah. Here parents of guest families could enjoy their beer or G & T and conversation while the kids bombed each other in the pool. It was an oasis where everything seemed perfect.

By my early twenties cracks emerged in that perfection to reveal a more complicated life. The West End became the scene of love and passion lost and rediscovered. Sufficiently different now, it is as if the hotel room door has closed on those memories and the exterior is now almost unrecognizable. It cannot possibly be the same place. It must have been a dream.

Mitlykhan in the Monsoon

EARLY JULY 1967

MITLYKHAN ESTATE DRAPES OVER THE hillside of the south end of the Baba Budan Giri, home of coffee in India. In 1670 AD Saint Baba Budan smuggled seven coffee beans out of Mocha, Arabia after his pilgrimage to Mecca. Beans strapped to his torso, he returned to Chikmagalur District in Karnataka, India and planted them. Today this is a flourishing coffee growing area, part of which belonged to my father and his business partner, a Scotsman named Alexander.

One monsoon morning we set out before 8 am to travel 58 kilometers from Kerkiecoondah Estate in the hills at Balanoor, which was home for me, across the valley of paddy fields, dene and jungle, to the Baba Budan Giri to Mitlykhan Estate for the weekend. It was a cold wet morning as we loaded the Willy's Jeep parked in the carport, as if we were heading out to cottage country for the weekend, except that the Jeep was loaded with food and supplies for three people, for two days, plus a 50lb sack of rice for the estate labourers. My father – Mike drove. Alex sat in the passenger seat. At 9 years of age, I was shoehorned into the back, with all the necessities for the trip. The rear and side canvas doors were rolled shut with small ventilation spaces at the driver's door so that exhaust fumes weren't sucked into the back of the vehicle. My mother waved us goodbye:

"Drive carefully Mike and look after Charlie. See you all Sunday night." She kissed Dad, then me, then waved us off. This journey took about four hours and was a weekly trip for Dad, but not for me and when I was not at home I assumed that my mother always accompanied him. The Jeep isn't big enough for four people and all the stuff, so mother stayed at home. At that age what else would I think was her reason for not coming with us to Mitlykhan? This is how I remember that trip to 'Mitly'.

The roads are fine till we reach the paddy fields where the earth baked tracks of summer have deteriorated into what seemed like muddy ice rinks in the monsoon. The Jeep bounces and slides along the road with Dad getting a work out, swiveling the steering wheel this way and that to keep the Jeep moving forward. The rain continues to pour down, the windscreen wipers slap left and right barely able to keep the window clear. There is no conversation. This kind of driving requires 100% concentration and instant reaction. As a passenger, I jostle around with each pothole or rock traversed, trying to soften the impact on whichever part of my body absorbed the jolt. The Jeep pulls up out of the valley into the jungle of the Forest Reserve.

For a few kilometers the road seems to smooth out but the density of the jungle vegetation creates a darkness, an eerie feeling. There is no one to be seen. The only sounds are the engine and constant deluge of rain falling on the canvas Jeep cover —tap, tap, tap, tap. Back into four-wheel drive, Dad gears down to navigate the small river raging across the road. He has done this many times before and gets us through.

"Well done Mike," says Alex, 65, who had spent his life in South India, mastered many languages and is a Renaissance man. Round the next corner, the back of the Jeep spins sideways. This time as Mike straightens it up, the front axle hits rock - crunch.

"Bloody hell. That's it," he says "We're stuck".

The men cautiously step out into the mud to see if indeed they might be able to push the Jeep off the rock. Through the plastic panel on the back canvas door, I can see Alex put his hands on the tailgate and gives a strong push. It barely moves.

"Charlie, hop out and see if that helps," Dad says. No change.

"Och Mike, one of us should walk to the Forest Ranger and see if he has the elephant in station and the other should walk up to the Estate with Charlie. Take the short cut up to the main Estate road and that will cut about 4 kliks off the walk."

"Right, I'll go to the Ranger and you take Charlie up to the bungalow. Not sure when I'll get home so go ahead and get settled in and I'll see you later," agrees Mike.

Alex and Dad close up the canvas doors and we set off with our ubiquitous black canvas umbrellas with the wooden handle, the men with their planters' boots and me in my brown canvas plimsolls, no socks. My feet start out dry but I know that by the time I reach the bungalow they will be squelching wet but not cold. The short cut is a narrow path through the jungle barely wide enough to allow the open umbrellas to pass. The rain drips constantly through the jungle canopy, on the leaves and our umbrellas. The wet leaves up to knee height occasionally brush against my leg and make me jump sideways to avoid whatever is trying to get me. Jungle walking in the rain is not fun. You never know what insect or 'thing' is going to leap on to your body or what creeper tentacle is going coil itself around you.

Alex carries a 'cutthie' with him, a small curved machete to cut back branches to make it easier for us to pass through. Thankfully after about 45 minutes of almost straight up hill, we are out on to the Estate road. Wide enough for one vehicle to travel, it is mostly a weedy, compacted gravel road rather than the muddy roads we'd been sliding along that morning.

"Charlie let's do a quick leech check," says Alex, but I was already thinking of the slimy ball of leeches that had probably already weaseled their way through the eyeholes of my shoes and attached themselves between my toes. The thing is, you never know whether they've made it into your shoes or not, till you take your shoes off at the end. The thin, pencil lead like creatures attach themselves as you walk along, then find their way into your shoes and down between your toes, where the feasting begins. They drink and become bloated with your blood to look more like black worms. Their parting gift - an itchy spot at the point of contact that irritates like a mosquito bite, for days.

This pause is also a few minutes respite to catch our breath after an almost vertical walk. At least from here we follow the road which zig-zags up the hill to the bungalow. It seems as though the rains have eased off. We are now in low, mist like clouds that are moving quickly. After about 10 minutes we fold up the umbrellas and use them as walking sticks. The silence is deafening. My father warned me to always listen and be aware of my surroundings when walking in or near the jungle because animals move with great stealth. The tiger, leopard, and even the bison will see you long before you know they are there. Most of the time they let you pass without you ever knowing they are there, but if they're hungry, or protecting their young, you'd better watch out. Till now Alex has been leading the way, but being unable to push these thoughts from my mind I need to walk a little ahead of him. I don't want to be stalked from behind. The road is wide enough for us to walk side by side so for a few minutes I keep an even pace. But still I feel the need to check over my shoulder. Gradually I pull a few steps ahead and hearing Alex's steady pace behind me is the comforting sound that reassures me I am safe. Somehow I don't think they will attack from the front.

"Charlie, look at this," Alex says as he points the tip of his folded umbrella at the hoof prints on the soft shoulder of the road. "Bison, looks like a big one. Probably came through here about half an hour ago. Keep your eyes open".

We continue on in silence till we reach a large tree on the side of the road. At the base of its trunk is a small plate with offerings, jasmine and marigold garlands. The red and white paint lines seen on the faces of swamis walking the towns are also painted on this tree.

"We must stop and offer puja," said Alex. "Labourers come here to offer prayers when they are working this section of the estate, for protection from snake, tiger or leopard attack. We should show our respects too".

With hands together in a prayer like fashion he bows his head and says "Namaste". I follow suit and pray that no tiger will jump out from behind me, no snake will coil around my legs and that we all get home before dark. "Namaste". We continue, me still a little ahead. Many switchbacks later, the coffee-drying ground comes into sight and on the hillside just above that, the Mitlykhan bungalow. The clouds have lifted and there is a small patch of blue sky. As we approach the bungalow, Raju, the house keeper greets us.

"Salaam Sahib, salaam Missy," he says, with a beaming smile. We both raise our right hand to salute him and return the greeting:

"Salaam Raju".

Alex continues to talk in Kannada, to ask him how he and his family are. Then after a few minutes of conversation, I am relieved to walk up the steps to the bungalow door. Feeling, wet with rain and sweat, thirsty and ready to sit down I want to change into dry clothes but realize I have to wait till Dad arrives for that change of clothes.

"Back to the boiler house Charlie and let's do a leech count," says Alex.

Alex and I sit on the bench in front of a large petrol drum, which contains water, a pipe leading in for cold water and one leading out for hot. The wood fire burns red under the drum. We peel off our shoes. I pull apart my big toe from the next one then continue, one, ...two...three. Using a small cloth for traction, I wrestle off the slimy leeches one by one. Black and fat, I toss them into the fire.

"I had 9, Uncle, how many did you have?" Alex was not my relative but in India all adults are "uncle" or "aunty" to children, and children seem to be children forever.

"Mmm you must have sweet blood – I only had 5!"

Back in the bungalow we sit on the verandah, each with a blanket wrapped around our shoulders. Raju brings us each a cup of hot chai – and the best ever plate of banana chips. Warming my hands around the cup, I stare out over the drying ground and remember one Christmas spent here during the picking season when it was covered with coffee beans. Many seasonal workers come during picking time including the roaming Lumbini from the north. Those evenings are often filled with song and dance in the gypsy tradition, accompanied by the rhythmical clicking sticks beating the rhythm, mirror covered skirts swirling and flickering in the firelight. And evening walks up along the ridge beyond the tree line, behind the bungalow, but not on this trip.

"When will Dad be here?"

"A wee while yet. Depends on how much help he was able to find. Don't worry lass, your father will sort it out and be here soon," says Alex in his warm Scottish accent.

I worry that Dad will need help and have no way to tell us. The Estate office has a landline: Panderavalli 44, but in the monsoon, the phone rarely works due to trees falling on the lines. It isn't working today. Once again my ears are fine tuned for any noise but in particular I am listening for the sounds of the Jeep grinding its way up the switchbacks. The gearing down around the corner then acceleration up out of the corner. Finally I hear it.

"Uncle I think I can hear the Jeep. Can you?" I ask.

It is dusk, must be around 5:45 pm. The cicadas are tuning up, making their loud noise like over amplified grasshoppers. The Jeep engine rumbling in the distance, gets louder and eventually Dad sounds the horn. The Jeep rounds the front of the bungalow, pulls to a gentle stop, the diesel engine silent. Out steps Dad.

"Well done Mike, let's find the Scotch and celebrate. Tell us what happened," says Alex as he helps unload the Jeep. Quicker than you can imagine we have everything out of the Jeep and into the bungalow including a polished wooden box that my father hands to me to carry up the steps and place on the verandah table next to Alex. He opens it up and takes out the two crystal Scotch glasses. Mike pours the Glenfiddich. I have more tea. We raise our glasses – and cup - "Cheers" clink, clink, clunk.

With the sun down, kerosene lanterns are lit. The drip, drip of rain resumes. I go to wash and change into some warm, dry clothes. One bucket of hot water is delivered to the bathroom from the boiler house. After my bucket bath, I tear off pieces of toilet paper and attach these scraps with my spit to each leech bite to stop the bleeding. I can recognize the distinctive, smell of Flit, which had been sprayed to deter the mosquitoes. It is 8:30 pm as we sit down at the table and drink hot tomato soup with croutons, which Dad has crisped up over the kitchen fire and eat warm cheese and bacon quiche dipped into Tobasco sauce, all prepared by my mother for this trip. Then a few mosquitoes start to whine around. Moths dive-bomb into the bright light of the lantern and fall clumsily onto the table. Even though I am now in dry clothes the dampness of the monsoon evening blows though the iron lattice screens surrounding the semi-enclosed verandah, where windows would normally be. Architectural relics from a time when those tigers and leopards would not hesitate to enter the building in search of food if no barrier was there to prevent them. A climate too hot to completely enclose the building with glass windows, these metal lattices also provide natural ventilation.

Feeling tired and looking forward to snuggling into a dry bed with woolen blankets, laid on the floor, I get a strong, loving hug from Dad, then head for bed. As my eyes close I hear the voices of Dad and Alex blur into sounds not words, I'm waiting for the hum of mosquitoes. Eventually the heavy rain drowns out any other sounds before I slip into the sleep of exhaustion.

2015

Now I think I understand why my mother wasn't on this week-end trip. But did she hate it so much that she wanted to be on her own rather than here, with us? Maybe the thought of battling through feet deep mud, fighting mosquitoes and the overall dampness of the monsoon in this simple house with baked cowpat floors and a wooden fire to cook on was just too much for her to deal with. Or maybe there just wasn't enough room in the Jeep for one more person?

Early Morning Ride

MAY 1981

"BUGGER" SHELAGH CURSED, "WE'VE GOT a flat". We were returning from Hassan with veterinary supplies for the horses and had turned off the local road from Balupet onto the track that took us across the dene to the thoroughbred stud farm – The Byerly Stud. It was early afternoon and there was no one around but the two of us. Shelagh got the manual from the glove box and in the middle of this empty grassland we started to read how to change a tire on this black 1960s Mercedes. She read the directions and I changed the tire. Her fingers were bent with arthritis and the pain of pressure on her fingers was too much to endure. It was hot and I was sweating with every doubled handed push and pull to release each lug nut. Within 40 minutes we had it beat but still with four kilometers of rutted road to travel.

After I graduated from University in Wales, I went to work for Shelagh and Fred who lived in the District adjacent to where my parents lived in Karnataka. Fred knew my father because they were both coffee planters. Shelagh lived for her horses and ran the farm on the side, while Fred, a former cavalry officer, managed the coffee estate. Then finally he retired from coffee planting and they were able to focus all their energies on the horses. As a couple they tended to draw young people into their lives as apprentices to learn about all aspects of breeding horses. They were recognized experts. Fred also had dairy cattle and a very small plot for coffee. During the monsoons of high school, I always spent a few weeks on the Farm.

Now that I was working on the farm seven days a week, I was woken at 5:30 am and in the stables by 6 am. The farm was home to 20 horses altogether, including a dapple grey, muscular stallion, whose pedigree was as exotic as his sire's name – Zedan. After an early morning review of the horses in the stable to make sure all were healthy, been fed, groomed and ready to go out into the paddock, occasionally I would ride òne of their mares out for exercise, though not one of their clients' prize winning mares. The early morning was the best time to ride, before the heat of the day made riding a penance and was the most magical time of the day.

This morning I had arranged to ride over to a friend's house across the valley for her excellent masala dosa breakfast. Shelagh and Fred had known her since she was a child but I had only known her for a few years. It had been a month since we'd seen each other. Shanti had been to Bangalore and returned so it was time to catch up. She and I met in Bangalore three years before, through a mutual friend, when we attended a Bangalore Club Diwali event. After the party, eight of us went to the Ashoka Hotel at 2 am for coffee before returning home. There I met her Dev. They were truly wrapped up in their own world and radiating happiness. Yes I was a little envious that I had not found an equally doting partner yet but at the same time acknowledged I was really enjoying everything else about life at that moment. Compromise is supposedly the key to a successful partnership, but I was still trying to define 'compromise' as there is a lot I didn't want to give up. Shanti seemed to have everything and give up nothing. How did she do that? But that was then. Now she is a widow and working hard to continue the successful coffee plantation Dev had inherited.

Riding out isn't like a walk in the park because you have to be constantly aware of your surroundings and anticipate anything that might spook the mare. No time for daydreaming. On this morning I rode Windsor. A rather leggy mare, 16 hands, and a little more relaxed than many but her thoroughbred blood lines meant she'd always be a little skittish. Once the syce – Krishnan, had saddled her up and handed me the reins I greeted her:

"Hello girl, how are you this morning? Ready for a ride out?" I rubbed her forehead, patted her neck, put the reins over her head and with a leg up from Krishnan, we were ready. Then we set off from the stables, down the farm track and out

onto the grassland scattered with copses that always held a surprise — birds flying out of the trees, rabbits darting back to cover — activity that kept Windsor alert and acutely aware of her surroundings.

It was about 7:00 in the morning. Even though I knew the route, there was a sense of excitement about leaving the security of the farm and heading out cross-country. The air was still, an early morning mist hung in the air. Along the fence line the filigreed handiwork of spiders glistened with dewdrops under the early morning sun. Windsor walked with purpose and I could feel her anticipation, that there was something unfamiliar with being beyond the paddock boundary. I could sense that she was a little uneasy: her gait was still more of a staccato movement and she swished her tail in agitation in this environment, so I talked her through her uneasiness. We had done this route before but not for a while.

As we walked down through the paddy fields by the river, the snowy egrets looked like statues, standing still, stalking their breakfast in the watery ground beneath them. Windsor's gait rocked my hips from side to side and the muffled sound of hoof beats clopped on the caked earth, her occasional snort and toss of her head were all signs that she too was embracing the day. The increasing cacophony of grassland birds greeted us as we reached the small stream in the valley. She stopped. I immediately gathered up the reins, squeezed my calves against her body to urge her forward: I let her back her up a few paces, then she stretched out her head indicating she wanted to put her muzzle into the water. I moved her forward and loosened the reins allowing her muzzle to touch the water; she took a drink, relaxed, and was ready to step further into the stream, and across to the other side. We continued along the track between the rice fields up to the boundary of Shanti's coffee estate. As we came closer to the boundary gate we could hear the field crew talking and laughing on their way to the assigned plot for the morning work and the rhythmical ringing of a brass bell. Windsor's ears were twitching as she could hear the sounds but not see the people. I knew that the sound of the bell meant that Reenu was also working today. The forest elephant in this district, she was contracted out to move felled trees or do any heavy lifting needed by the local farmers. With her ambling pace her bell had a distinct rhythmic sound, which I recognized, but Windsor did not.

The boundary gate was three bamboo poles that slid into holes on gateposts on both sides of the track. I dismounted and slid the reins over Windsor's head while I lifted the poles down at one end so that Windsor could navigate over them and once closed, I remounted. Not sure how Windsor was going to react when she saw Reenu, I gathered up the reins to prepare for her surprised reaction and gave her a few gentle pats on her neck. We rounded the corner.

Windsor stopped immediately, raised her head and started to back up, prancing as she liked to do. *"Easy, easy now Windsor, Reenu is not going to hurt you."* I patted her on her neck as my legs signaled her forward.

The work crew were predominantly women and all huddled together, one trying to stand behind the other, the whites of their eyes flashing nervous glances at each other, while the few men just backed into the coffee bushes. They were not as familiar with horses as they were with elephants. As Reenu, ridden by her mahout, and Windsor drew parallel, we stopped so that Windsor could smell Reenu. Reenu took the opportunity to snack some leaves from the roadside with her trunk. Windsor was clearly tentative, but then her curiosity became stronger than her fear. She let out a soft snort as her muzzle softly brushed the leathery skin on the side of Reenu's belly. Reenu turned her head. Her little eye glanced at Windsor; ears gave a gentle flap. Her mahout confirmed to her that this 'other four legged thing' was no threat to her.

There, not so bad after all Windsor, is it? Once the sniffing was over I thanked the mahout, waved 'Salaam' and moved on.

We continued up through the estate, the white coffee blossoms in full bloom and jasmine-like fragrance intoxicating. A gentle breeze whispered through tall casuarina trees and extended the coolness of early morning. Rounding the corner, I could see the bright pink and yellow bougainvillea, which marked the edge of Shanti's colourful garden. She must have heard us coming:

"Hi Charlie, you made it! How was the ride? Come breakfast is almost ready, you must be hungry," she called and waved. I rode up to the verandah steps, dismounted and walked Windsor over to a stall for her to wait, with some lucerne as a treat, while Shanti and I caught up.

"When did you get back from Bangalore who did you see there, did you go shopping, did you see a movie?" I needed to ask all my questions while I had the chance as Shanti was quite the talker once she got the stage. She'd always been a talker, but when Dev was here she had a conversational ebb and flow to give him a voice amongst friends. Now at twenty five, she was a widow and filled that space that once was Dev's. She embraced being a young, female, coffee planter, something that had really rocked this essentially male community. Dev was the love of her life, not an arranged marriage and she now dedicated herself to carrying on the family estate, as Dev would have wanted.

"Ya, ya, ya Charlie I did all the usual AND I met VJ at the Bangalore Club. He's visiting his brother and he asked if you were in town as well. He's a nice guy and I've known his family since I was about 10, I think. Are you interested?" she asked. Whoah – I hadn't anticipated that question. Yes, I did like him, he liked horses, was a good rider and we were both in Newmarket, England at the same time last year at the yearling sales. But I was not ready to have this conversation and ignored her question.

"Shanti – who else did you see?" I asked.

"As I was leaving the accountant's office, Manu was just arriving. He seemed in a hurry but did ask me for dinner that evening, and I accepted. He is a good friend and knew Dev since they were at College. It's great to be able to talk shop with him as well. My parents think he would be perfect for me! But the bar has been set high and it will take me a while to understand that I'll never find another Dev," she replies.

Apart from the decidedly girly updates on these trips to the city, she always included the meetings with the bank manager, the accountant, suppliers of fertilizer, pulp machinery or any other coffee related equipment. There was invariably a new merchant who didn't realize who they were dealing with and would try to rip her off. After all, what would she know about fertilizer prices? Most vendors knew who Shanti was and gave her the respect she deserved.

The masala dosa was delicious, crisp and hot, served with my favourite coconut chutney. The potatoes were cooked just right with the perfect balance of mustard seed and tumeric, wrapped in the blanket of a warm rice pancake, moist on the inside and crisp on the outside!

Time to go, we both had to get back to work. The warm hug marked the end of this visit.

"Bye Shanti, thank you, that was a great dosa," I said.

"My pleasure – and let me know what you think about VJ!" she said with a big smile.

By now the sun was up but still not the blistering heat of mid-day. East of the coffee estate are a few kilometers of relatively flat, open land, just perfect for a gallop before turning north and heading home. From the moment we passed through Shanti's Estate gate Windsor's pace picked up to a brisk walk and I could sense that she was wound up like a spring. With little encouragement the spring unwound. I could feel the surge of adrenaline within me, the warm air across my face and the rapid beat of Windsor's hooves at the gallop. I let her run till she stared to slow down then pulled her up to a walk to turn around and we headed towards the local village then back across the grassland to arrive home in a circular route. As we walked through the village, daily duties were well underway: a women bent over sweeping the ground in front of her house; toddlers peering through the doorway, a dog casually cleaning himself, a gaggle of girls on their way to the well to fill their water pots. They paused when they saw us walking by. We greeted each other with 'Salaam' and continued on with our daily purpose. On leaving the village, we passed two young boys herding their goats and cattle out to graze for the day but Windsor seemed to barely notice the bleeting, bustling herd. She was more focused on getting back to the stable.

We arrived back at the stables where I dismounted and gave the reins to Raju. Windsor's breathing had returned to normal after the gallop although she was clearly sweating. I gave her a few firm, thankful pats on her neck: *Good job Windsor.* I checked each lower leg for any nicks to her skin and each hoof to ensure no stones were caught in her hooves. She rubbed the side of her head against my shoulder and let out a deep whinny as Raju took her to the stable to remove the tack, rub her down, give her a drink, then take her out to the paddock for the rest of the morning. I walked back to the bungalow for coffee and a break, reflecting on Shanti's question and once again thanking the universe for placing me here in god's country.

Shanti didn't ride so we only met monthly but somehow it was comforting to know that she was across the valley should anything untoward happen. The phone worked on most occasions but this was pre internet and cell phone days. Our friendship strengthened — two young women living unique lives, filled with the contrasts of beauty and brutality in a landscape of adventure. A landscape where Shanti was at home and in control but one in which I was a mere dilettante, a white face in a brown world. I didn't have the purpose and drive Shanti had, neither did I have her broken heart. What was my direction? All I knew for sure was that I was postponing the inevitable — India was my home but not for long. I didn't want to leave but in my heart knew it was inevitable.

It was 9 am and I joined Shelagh for a coffee while she ate breakfast and we discussed what was on deck for the rest of the day.

Dinner at the Kadur Club

THE GLASS EYES OF THE tiger stare down from the whitewashed wall in the Kadur Club lounge. The big cat's mouth open in a snarl, its head resting on a small shelf below its chin and the body of the skin pinned up on the wall. This was the trophy that represented a time well before my father's experience but certainly within my grandfather's. There is no plaque to say who shot this tiger or when. Tigers are both feared and revered, the very symbol of India and that was one of the reasons Tippu Sultan of Mysore was called Tippu the Tiger. The white-washed pillars on the verandah are architectural statements, remnants of the days when there were many English coffee and tea planters in the district.

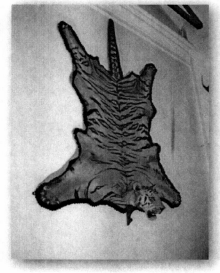

It is 2007, 20 years since I was last here, and I was returning here with Rachel, a friend I'd met in Bangalore when we were in our 20's – around he same time that I met Shanti, and who had continued to live in India after I left. This evening we stopped at the Club en route to Kerkiecoondah Estate where I had spent some of my childhood. We would stay for a few days hiking.

The drive took about 7 hours from Bangalore so stopping at the Kadur Club was an opportunity to stretch, get a bite to eat and just take a break from driving. Rachel had called a few days before to confirm our arrival this evening. From the lounge we walk into the dining room, another imposing space with tall ceilings and walls covered with more trophies: huge bison heads, deer and a few water colour paintings of race horses in the parade ring. The dining room table is a long, polished, teak table to seat 32 but this evening set for two. As we pull out the heavy chairs to sit down the sound of wood dragged on the waxed red floor, echoes around the room. The Bearer, dressed in whites and a white turban but with no shoes, shuffles towards us.

"Good evening Madam, shall I serve dinner?" asked the Bearer.

"Yes, please. Michael is that you?" I asked hesitantly.

"Yes Madam," replied Michael. He had aged significantly. He was one of four Bearers which included his father, at the Club when I was growing up.

"How is your father, your family?" I asked.

"Father passed, 10 years now, my mother passed last year. But I have my wife, one daughter and one grandson. So I am very lucky and I still work here".

"I'm sorry you've lost your parents. Your father was always very kind to me when I was a child and visiting the Club. He always brought me fresh sweet-lime juice just before I had my hair cut on the back verandah. I hated the barber, but the sweet lime juice must have sweetened me to behave."

"I will bring the soup first. One minute please".

We started with the Club classic - consommé soup, followed by Madras Curry with papadams. The plates are white with a worn and barely visible gold club crest on the edge. The cutlery, rather large and heavy silver plate, imported from Sheffield, is dulled by the years of service. We don't talk much through dinner. After five hours on the road we were hungry.

"Have you finished Madam?" asked Michael.

"Yes thank you Michael that was very good."

"Did Madam see the Presidents Board outside the Billiard Room? It has the names of all Presidents since the beginning of the Club."

"Mr. Keene is there", he said referring to my father, "Also Mr. Graham," a close friend of his.

"Also Mr. Cariappa and Mr. Sethna." Michael smiles and leads the way to the verandah, unbolting the tall wood and glass panel doors. Like many Brits post World War Two, my parents chose to live and work in a place that had been under British rule but was now independent. A place where English was spoken and used in business and bureaucracy interchangeably with Hindi and the local language - Kannada. I am one of four children and as was the convention, we were all sent back to boarding school in England.

Movement between England and India was easy but it took time. When my parents first set sail for India it was by ship, first past the Cape, South Africa, then shortened up via the Suez Canal once that was opened. By the time I was 'tooing and froing' between home and school it was by plane, from London, via Geneva, Frankfurt or Rome – Dubai - Bombay then Bangalore. When I reached high school it was London-Bombay on a 747 and to Bangalore on an Airbus. This trip I had flown directly from London to Bangalore on a 777. So yes it only took 10 hours to fly there from London but since the horrendous events of 9/11 - the fall of the Twin Towers, a visa is now required in your passport before you can get on a plane to India, if you are not an Indian citizen.

Rachel was not from Chikmagalur – the District that was pivotal in voting Indira Ghandi to her role as the third Prime Minister for a second term. Her family owned property in a neighbouring District – Hassan. There was a similar Planters Club there too, the Munzerabad Club in Sakleshpur. These Clubs are scattered across South India and those in urban centers remain social hubs for planters who live out of town and who can afford the annual fees.

It is 8 o'clock, time to move on as we still have two hours driving to get to the Estate. Rachel and I walk towards the kitchen to say good bye to Michael and sign the chit. She gives him a tip and we turn to walk the length of the dining hall and out to the car. The sound of our shoes squeaking across the polished floor is our exit. The Club had been a lively venue for Independence Day parties, Diwali and Christmas as well. It was the social hub for coffee and tea planters in Chikmagalur District. People who rarely saw each other once out on their estates as in any farming community. Now most planters live in Bangalore and return to the estates as needed. The roads are wider, smoother, making for faster driving and a shorter trip. There seemed no need to stay on the estate all year round.

"The Toyota Highlander pulled out of the Club driveway, with Rachel – a more cautious driver – taking over the night section to the Estate. I had driven the section from Bangalore to the Club.

"Well that was a trip for you Charlie. It is amazing how Michael still remembers you and your family. People like him must really have a colourful history in their memories. Imagine him writing a book. I bet he'd have some stories, if the Kadur Club was anything like Munzerabad," says Rachel.

"Right," I acknowledge in an almost melancholy way.

" You know more about your family history in India than I do about mine! I remember when I visited you in England a few years ago at your parents' cottage there was a large Gainsborough like painting hung on the landing. Remind me what was her connection to India?" she asks.

"Her name is Jane Harris and she married Alfred Thomas Keene, my great, great, great, grandfather. Jane's brother was George Harris, First Lord of Seringapatam and Mysore. That is where our familial connection with India started. But you won't believe this…at 94 my mother finally sold the cottage. She had lived there, alone, for ten years after my father died. I always remember that year because I went back to England in September to spend a week with my mother, trying to accept that my father had passed. I was due to fly out of Heathrow the morning the Twin Towers in New York were destroyed. The painting was put up for auction in England about ten years later and bought by Jane's surviving family – the descendants of the First Lord of Seringapatam and Mysore." I reply filling in the blanks for Rachel.

"I have no idea about my family tree beyond my great grandfather but I'll bet we must have had a relative in the Seringapatam wars. What if we were on opposite sides of this argument?" asks Rachel provocatively.

"Well they could just as easily have fought with the British as so many did. Both our ancestors could have fought under the command of Colonel Wellesley, who then became the Duke of Wellington. What if your relative was one of those who discovered the body of Tippu after he was slain in 1799?" I question.

"Ya, ok I'll go with that but I'm going to check into this when I get back to Bangalore. I'm really curious to know if we have that historical connection. Your parents were married before they came to Bangalore, no?"

"No, they came to India independent of each other and while in Bangalore they fell in love, then married there. I don't give my mother the acknowledgement she deserves for her adventurous spirit and signing up to come to Bangalore as a nurse in the Queen Alexandra's Nursing Corps just at the end of the Second World War. She must have been in her early twenties. It was a very lonely life for her as a young woman married to a young tea planter in the middle of nowhere South India." I reflect.

"My mother's family is from Kerela and my father's from Madras but they too met in Bangalore as both sides of the family had moved there when my parents were children. I'm not sure why they sent me off to high school in England other than it was my entrée to Cambridge University," said Rachel.

"See Rachel you are more English than I am! When you were a kid did your parents take you to Belur, Halebede, Sravenabelagola, Sringeri?" I ask. I often wondered if the 'templing' was something only foreigners did.

"Not so much. I remember going to Sravenabelagola. My god the size of that towering statue of Gomateshwara all carved out of one piece of granite," she said.

"Yeah and my sisters and I used to giggle about this size of his penis, it must have been about 5 feet tall." I add.

"Us too, although we were always very discreet about it around my parents!" she smiles. Sravanabelagola was a quieter place where as a child I felt more relaxed. There always seemed to be a sense of overwhelming chaos in the towns surrounding the other two temples, so many people jostling around, child beggars who flocked to us the moment we stepped out of the car, following, running in front of us and shoving each other out of the way to gain their place of prominence. Often quite a claustrophobic experience for me, which was relieved once we entered the temple gates unlike the wilderness of the Estate.

It is dark outside no light except for the headlights of the SUV as Rachel carefully drives along the winding road up through the jungle areas and past other coffee estates. It is difficult driving to avoid the potholes and not knowing what might be lying in the road around the next corner. At least it isn't raining. There is a lull in the conversation.

"You remember Samir who used to hang out with us in Bangalore, he went to the States for grad school, MBA right?" Rachel enquired.

"Yes, I actually met up with him in Berkley once when I was living in Santa Cruz. He was having a hard time deciding whether to return to India or break from the family and stay in the US. I'm assuming he's married by now but I haven't heard from him for years," I responded. As teenagers Samir and I spent hours in art galleries in Bangalore. Whenever there was an exhibition of the latest local artist we were there. Whenever he needed an easy win at squash, I was the selected partner. Whenever I needed an exhilarating motorbike ride, he was my go to guy. It wasn't until about three years after I had been living in California that I discovered that Samir was living in Berkley. We met for a day of coffee, walking and conversation. He was clearly unhappy, I suggested he go home and be with his family while he figures this out. Did I give him the wrong advice? Another silence before Rachel replies.

"Well he did return to Bangalore but that was about 12 years ago. I didn't see him but a friend passed on the details. Not sure if you're ready for this. He died about three months after he returned."

"Oh my god. I had no idea. What happened?" I ask.

"Well that's a little uncertain. The family says he passed in his sleep, he just didn't wake up. But, I've also heard that he overdosed."

"No, I don't believe it," I said in disbelief.

"Well that's what most people say, but other sources say that they knew Samir was really depressed and possibly OD'd on something. There was no autopsy so no one knows for sure."

"Wow, is there anything else you want to put on the table while I'm in shock?"

"No. Everyone else we used to hang out with is either married with kids, divorced with kids or widowed."

"Samir is the first friend of mine who has died. It feels strange. I don't think it has fully sunk in. No one told me," I say in disbelief with anger and sadness.

"Charlie, when it happened we were all busy in our own worlds, you in California, so far away. We hadn't been in contact for years. I'm not going to call you out of the blue to tell you your friend from a long time ago has just died. But I'm really happy you came to visit now. I haven't done a trip like this away from kids and Praveen for years."

"So, Rachel – let's not be so distant after this visit. It is easier to stay connected these days," I say. Rachel stops the car while the night watchman opens the gates. Then drives the last few kilometers to the bungalow where we will stay for a few days. It was a clear night and the stars were bright in the dark sky.

"Rach – I learned to drive here in the Willy's Jeep. My father gave me lessons at 12. I remember being really scared at first then grew to love the challenge of navigating around those muddy old roads. Thanks for driving the last bit." It was past 10 o'clock and both of us are tired. The house-keeper welcomes us into the bungalow, makes sure we have all we need for the night and leaves.

"Looks like they have made the guest room ready for you. I'll be in the room next door, which used to be my room when I was a kid. Good night. I'll see you at breakfast" I say as we hug each other.

"Welcome home Charlie," says Rachel.

I'm tired and jetlagged from the long journey from London. I open the door to the bathroom and descend the three steps to where the metal bathtub, hand basin and toilet are, just as I remember. As I unpack my toothbrush and toothpaste I decide I'll skip that for tonight and just go to bed. I put my head on the pillow, remembering being here as a child, the warm hug of my mother and kiss good night. Listening to the frogs and occasional jackal call. Within seconds I am asleep.

Tippu's Drop

AUGUST 2009

BLR - BANGALORE AIRPORT AT dawn. From the years of flying I knew the airport codes for most places where my flight stopped between LHR and BLR. Memorizing these codes came easily and continued even as I travelled for work. VJ and I saw each other simultaneously – hands waving above our heads through the throng of taxis, porters and people arriving off the Lufthansa 777 from LHR.

"Charlie you're looking great and you're crazy. No bags then. We only have 24 hours before I have to bring you back to the airport. Too bad you had that mix up with your visa. I had so much planned for the week and now we have just one day. Let's have a coffee over here then get going," VJ invited.

"It's so good to see you too VJ – you haven't changed, well mostly. It must be about seven years since we were in Yosemite. Yeah in hindsight I should have thought that I needed a visa for India. Seems like being born here carries no weight these days. 9/11 changed more than we realize," I said. Once the sun began to appear and the coffee had kicked in VJ was anxious to move on.

"Come, we must go before the sun gets too high!" he urged "Up to Tippu's Drop, all 1,175 steps."

This was Tippu Sultan's fortress, his cool escape from the heat of the plains in the summer. The Sultan of Mysore from 1750-99, is legendary for many reasons but in this location in particular because his prisoners were pushed to their death over a sheer 600 meter drop. The shallow steps to the top were carved out of a granite monolith, one of many strewn across the surrounding barren plains as if God had taken a handful of rocks and like dice, rolled them across the earth.

It was about an hour's drive in the cool morning air to the base of the climb. Having not seen each other for such a long time we had surprisingly little to say. I looked out the window, feeling the effects of lack of sleep and jetlag mixed with the excitement of coming home after 20 years. The car sped passed ploughed fields, villages waking up, children walking to school or herding their goats out to graze the countryside. We stopped for a few minutes to explore a small walled cemetery remembering British soldiers from generations past. It was hard to read the inscriptions on the tombstones as vines were creeping over the tops of the stones to meet the small shrubs growing up from the base. A solitary yew tree stood in the middle and the offset opening in the surrounding wall prevented the cattle and goats from entering. On to the next village we stop at a small Temple, leaving our sandals by the gate. No one in sight, we strolled around the courtyard enjoying the cool stone floor underfoot, the light fragrance of incense and the random calls of the village rooster announcing the new day. The mellow gold of the sunrise shone on the sculptures in homage.

"I haven't been to this temple before but it reminds me of many my father took me to over the years," I said as we walked back to the car. VJ drove on to their next stop, a narrow side road with barely enough room to park the car on the side. The starting point of the steps up to Tippu's Drop. VJ reversed the car off to the side of the road under a tree to try and keep it cool for our return. We set off up the steps faster than was necessary and found the conversation ebb and flow, punctuated by stops in silence to catch our breath, to admire the view. I wondered why our lives travelled in parallels, across continents, over decades. An elderly swami, dressed in white, stooping and bow legged, passed us in silence with his slow but steady pace, a walk he does twice a day. He made it look so easy, not the least out of breath. Once we reached the top, perspiring and my heart pounding with every last step; the cool, moist air of the cloud felt refreshing. Our arrival upset the tranquility of the moment as monkeys burst into a flurry of screeches, which set the bulbuls and mynahs calling, creating a cacophony in this microcosm of jungle. Then quieted down again. We wandered around the fort, seemingly alone.

"Over here. Look its Tippu's Drop," called VJ. Come carefully. It gets a little slippery near the edge," VJ cautioned me. He held out his hand to guide me towards the edge.

"I'm not good with heights so don't let go" I said as I cautiously moved closer. We peered over the wall by the Drop. As I leaned over I began to feel a little dizzy. Am I falling? Is this real or are we characters in an E. M. Forster novel, I thought. The incident at the Marabar Caves flashed through my mind. Am I finally acknowledging there is more to this relationship or am I confusing the emotion with the exhilaration from the hard ascent and the giddiness of exertion? VJ was no Aziz, nor was I Ms. Quested, but this was a 21st Century Passage to India.

Sightseeing in Seringapatam

NOVEMBER 2011

THIS NOVEMBER MORNING, LIKE SO many mornings before, I am taking the bus to work, in Vancouver – beautiful British Columbia. 'Next Stop Arbutus' announces the digital conductor on the #9 bus east bound. I close my eyes as the storefronts slip by and the bus sways along the route from stop to stop. My mind drifts to memories of a warmer place and time, my visit last August to Bangalore, India and a few other key places in my life: Mysore, where I was born, Seringapatam where my ancestor fought in the Battle of Seringapatam and Hassan, from where I left 27 years ago. And Tippu's Summer Palace, where I unexpectedly receive an answer to a question I had not yet articulated to myself.

SRIRANGAPATANA STATION, SOUTH INDIA: AUGUST 2011

We watch the train slowly pull into the sweeping curve of the Srirangapatana station from across the Cauvery River bridge. The First and Second Class coaches roll by as the screeching breaks bring the train to a halt. Within seconds passengers are pouring off the train as others are elbowing their way to a seat.

"Banana, banana, banana," shouts a young boy walking on the platform alongside the train, eager for customers.

Passengers on board wave their hands through the window bars to beckon him closer to buy, while boarding passengers push suitcases and families in through the doors. Those disembarking are making sure all the luggage and family are off the train. That nothing or no one is left behind. Porters on the platform load sacks on their heads, suitcases and bundled belongings in each hand and under each arm. Others have nothing and walk through the station gate into the countryside beyond.

The platform clears and as the last coach pulls through the station the Conductor, waving his green flag, blows a shrill blast on his whistle, steps back on board and the train is gone. A scrawny dog resumes his position curled up on the mat in front of the ticket master's door. The platform is empty.

"That's it Charlie, let's walk over to Bailey's Dungeon," says VJ.

"Wait let me take your photo, there against the wall". In large black letters painted on a whitewashed wall reads "ABANDONED". We had not abandoned each other over the years but perhaps it was more a case of 'Lost and Found'. Maybe others had abandoned him — that is his journey, not mine. VJ and I remained friends throughout our tumultuous lives since we were teenagers. We met when I was 18 and recently moved to Bangalore for college. He had completed his medical training and within two weeks was preparing to leave to work in Africa. During this time we had no intimate relationship but an understanding that maybe if there was more time, something would develop. There was no time, so we remained friends in a group of young people who hung out together. We met again briefly when I was at University in Wales and he was working in a Hospital in London. Then again in Santa Cruz, California, then Yosemite National Park with his wife and two daughters and me with my two children. And so these brief encounters have continued throughout our lives, never really going anywhere, but I have been trying to understand the meaning of our connection. Now we are both single again, back to the beginning, it was time to answer this question.

"Charlie you know that the Dungeon is part of the Fort of Seringapatam, built by Tippu Sultan in the 1780's for his prisoners", says VJ.

"Yes, my father brought me here when I was about 7. I'm not sure we even got out of the car but he told us we have a relative who fought against Tippu," I reply.

As I lean against the ramparts atop the dungeon, looking across the great Cauvery River, I can hear people walking my way, talking and laughing. They stop to chat with VJ who has drifted a few paces away from me. They work for a computer company in Bangalore and have taken the day off to see the historical sights of the Great Tippu.

"Come Charlie let's go over to the Gumbaz, Tippu's mausoleum," VJ says as he approaches me again. "It's about a ten-minute drive from here."

We get out of the Ambassador and walk towards the old woman in a sari who is guarding an increasingly large gathering of shoes. She gives us the almost toothless smile of a hockey player, puts her hands together and greets us with "Namaste". VJ and I remove our shoes. The dark grey clouds of monsoon are gathering above and shafts of sunlight beam down onto the decorative carvings of white marble of the building, almost as if their laser-like precision cut the filigreed artwork.

"Stop here a minute VJ, I can't see in this darkness," I whisper as I follow VJ into the room where Tippu's tomb rests. There is no artificial lighting. The stone floor is cool under my feet. A slight fragrance of incense wafts through the room. The silence of respect is heightened by the gentle breeze that slips through the doors and caresses our bodies as we enter. The clouds pass, sunlight streams through the door across the tombs of the great Tippu, his father and his mother. Pilgrims walk past, stop, bow, and then move on. As I stand here, inches away from Tippu's tomb I wonder if George Harris ever got this close to him. I have no idea where George is buried but for a few seconds I am standing next to the body of someone who was in the same place as George, at the same time, over two hundred years ago.

I look over to VJ and tilt my head pointing to the exit. We join up again by the shoes.

"One last stop for today –Tippu's Summer Palace?" suggests VJ.

"Sure," I say as we scan the shoes, looking for ours.

At the Palace, the humidity and warmth of the monsoon afternoon and the toll of sightseeing has slowed us down. The tranquility of the palace adds to the somnolent feeling. Lethargically, I lead the way up the steps onto the verandah where the walls are covered in large murals depicting scenes from Tippu's successful campaigns against the British. Somewhere on the ground in this sea of soldiers and horses are the heads of cavalrymen. This scene is from the 1780 battle of Pollier, the heads on the ground belonged to Colonel Baillie's men.

"See if you can find the heads," challenges VJ and never allowing myself to be outdone by him, I will find them. The painting, in the style of the Moghul masters, has rows of soldiers on horseback, in profile, heading towards the enemy. Most are turbaned with their swords drawn or holding what looks like a tall javelin. The horses are held in a tight rein, muscular necks arched, eyes often looking wild and nostrils flared, ready to charge again.

"I found two heads." I reply "And I've had enough VJ. Let's go back to the Club and get a beer." We walk to the front of the Palace, our pace still slow, close to each other, the backs of our hands occasionally touching. I stop and turn to VJ.

"Why did you bring me here today?" I ask. He turns to face me, gently cups his hands around the back of my neck and draws my forehead to rest on his. Then moves his left arm to reach across my back and hug my shoulder, drawing us closer.

"You have so much family history tied up in this country, Charlie. I wanted you to see this for yourself. I wanted you to understand that this is your home as much as mine. Your family's blood is in this soil. You belong here. I know that, but I wanted you to see, to feel it for yourself. Did nothing we saw today touch you?" asks VJ. I can hear emotion in his voice that I have never heard before.

"Yes, but it's history and may help me understand who I am, but doesn't have magical powers to hold me here. What would I do here anyway? I couldn't survive in Bangalore," I reply.

"City life in Bangalore is good. Besides, we could be together," he says.

"Wow VJ, it has taken you 25 years and three continents to say that to me," I exclaim. Is this too late? I put my arm casually around his waist. We walk in silence to the car. Hearing his words echo in my head and listening to my heart, I understand what the answer must be.

NOVEMBER 2011

Bing bong 'Next Stop Granville', my stop. I can't remember anything about what I've seen in the last 20 minutes except that I've just been with VJ. I get off the bus and hurry off down to the office and all that this world will bring me today.

The Tomb of Tippu Sultan lies here.

Meenu's Biryani

Snowflakes float down onto the balcony on this cold December morning. The sparkling snowcapped peaks of the North Shore are but shadows. It's Sunday in Vancouver. No rush off to work, no other pressing commitments except that today I decide to make biryani from Meenu's recipe. Meenu and her husband Ashok are close family friends in Bangalore. I first met Ashok when he came to work with my father on the Estate, as an apprentice, even though his family owned the property. Then he married Meenu. That seems like a long time ago. It is almost four months now, since I last visited them in Bangalore and followed Meenu around her kitchen, watching and scribbling in my red moleskine notebook, the details of how to make this favourite dish. It would have been circumspect to re-write the recipe later that evening, when I was there, but having missed that opportunity, I am just going to work from my note book and memory to see if I can recreate her delicious biryani. Yesterday I made a shopping list from those notes and felt assured that all the ingredients were in my kitchen. Now seems a perfect time to attempt to duplicate Meenu's biryani. I am almost ready to start cooking but as I gaze out my window in my Vancouver townhouse, I know the missing ingredient is the chatter from her kitchen, the warmth of being close to friends who know my history and who I have become, without feeling the need to explain everything. I spend a few more minutes staring out the window and remembering that evening in the Bangalore.

I have known Ashok and Meenu for almost 35 years although I haven't spent any time with them for the past 20. The family ties span two generations. During this last visit with them, I am rekindling friendships and blending in with their daily lives.

AUGUST 2011

Ashok and Meenu are a one-car family so Meenu always tries to get Ashok to do domestic errands on his way back from the office. Traffic is so bad here, that coming home then going out again with the car for groceries would just take too long. Meenu phones Ashok:

"Hi Ashok, Rohan and Deeks are at home for dinner this evening so I need you to pick up four large tomatoes and a loaf of bread on your way home. ... Okay, ...Okay... see you at 6:30."

Rohan, their youngest son married Deeks last year and are on the cusp of moving into their own apartment, which they have been renovating for weeks. Until then they will stay with Meenu and Ashok. Meenu has a modern kitchen, rectangular with cool polished stone floors and shiny marble countertops. The walls are lined with tall cupboards filled with a plethora of kitchen necessities but I'm almost sure only the things on the lowest shelves are used, as Meenu is diminutive in stature, though a goliath in spirit. Also an abundance of drawers filled with utensils, cutlery and the requisite 'sharp knife'. There is no dishwasher so the dish rack is always filled with crockery or pots and pans that have just been used and washed. The freezer is in the next room, in the laundry area, so there is frequent family traffic passing through the kitchen and conversations that ebb and flow in passing during meal prep time.

Within a few hours Ashok has returned home, Meenu has all the ingredients and is ready to start. She slices and caramelizes the onions, then adds grated ginger, diced garlic and two teaspoons of mild chili powder to the hot oil in the pan. After about five minutes she adds a sliced green chili, then the chops tomatoes and stirs gently. Just before that she chopped coconut and cashews in the blender with a little water to create a creamy paste.

"Did you know biryani is a dish from the Mughals, served in Delhi and Lucknow?" Ashok says as he passes through the kitchen to the fridge to get a soda water.

"It was easier to feed the thousands of soldiers a rice-based dish than individual chapattis or rotis with accompaniments. From there the Nawabs adapted the dish to their specific regions, with slight adjustments to spices, more chilies or less, cashew nuts or not, cooking the rice with the meat or separately."

Tonight I am going to learn how to cook the Malayali version of biryani. There is no written recipe to copy.

> *In a separate pan, sauté the chicken till sealed, stir in ½ cup of plain yoghurt and let simmer for 30 minutes, then add that to the tomato mixture and juice of ½ a lime. Add coriander and mint leaves.*

Rohan, is looking for his shirt: "Amma have you seen my green, stripped shirt? It's not in my cupboard. Did you wash it recently? I need it for this meeting tomorrow with Appa and this chap from Mumbai. Did Appa mention that he's interested in buying coffee to sell in Vancouver? That shirt is my favourite and I really want to wear it tomorrow," he mumbles as he walks from the laundry area through the kitchen to the dining room.

"I have the shirt with my ironing. I'll take care of it after dinner. Where's Appa, is he back yet?" Deeks inquires on her way to the dining room.

"He is hiding out in the bedroom watching CNN and relaxing, keeping clear of the kitchen for now. He'll come soon," Meenu assures, smiling.

"Tomorrow the TV is being delivered to our apartment and we can't decide which room to put it in. It is a big TV, 56" " Rohan smiles, "It will probably go in the bedroom".

> *Add half a cup of yoghurt and allow to cook slowly. Wait a minute — how many onions? How much ginger? How much garlic? When did the nut mixture go in?*

"Deeks did you look at the gas stoves after work today?" Meenu is anxious about the house blessing for Deeks and Rohan next week because they can't move into the new apartment till the blessing is done and that won't happen if they can't boil the milk to spill over. They must have a stove.

"Yes and we selected one which they'll also deliver tomorrow evening. So why don't you all come over after dinner tomorrow and help set all this up?"

> *In the rice add four cloves, four cardamoms and two pieces of cinnamon. Cook till rice is ready.*

Deeks sets the table with placemats and plates. I offer to get the cutlery.

"Well Charlie, you're welcome to do that but we don't need cutlery!" Her eyes sparkle as she smiles, reminding me that I am the only one this evening who needs to use cutlery. Deeks is more like a daughter in this family than the daughter in law that she is.

Ashok emerges and wants to know if he has time to make a phone call but Meenu suspects that will go well past when dinner is ready.

"Ashok, dinner is almost ready, just check that there is water on the table and glasses".

Add cooked rice and chicken in layers into a large serving dish, place in oven for about five minutes. Serve.

"Dinner's ready." She announces, and everyone converges on the table. The familiar silence of well-satisfied hunger takes over.

"Delicious," I comment enthusiastically.

"Meenu — something's missing." Observes Ashok. Silence at the table. Meenu looks at Ashok trying to guess what might be missing:

"I forgot the salt," she realizes.

December 2011

Ah yes, the salt, here it is.

I'm back in my kitchen in Vancouver making sure all the ingredients are on the kitchen counter. Will this biryani taste as good as Meenu's? Maybe, but the ingredient I am missing is Meenu and her family.

This vignette reminds me of a quote from Vikram Vij, Vancouver's very own celebrity chef *"Good food should not only be served with passion and love but with humility."*

From Home to Hampi

AUGUST 2012

"WE MUST LEAVE AT SIX o'clock. That means we must be in the car and ready to leave at six not waking up at six," says Ashok the night before, as he looks directly at Meenu.

This return trip to the coffee estate with them arrives filled with anticipation and a strong dose of sadness as I know this will likely be the last time I visit the Estate. I had fought with the desire to return for fear that everything would be so different now, that maybe I should just let those memories of childhood reign but perhaps I should 'just do it' as it might help me understand my current need to revisit the past. Travelling from Vancouver to Bangalore is a long and expensive journey but one I needed to do, but without my husband and children. Now that I had neither, the time seemed right. Family friends who own the Estate made this journey possible and the only way I would return. Knowing they are here provides reassurance, a blanket of care for me, as I am afraid of how I will react. Would this open up memories I had successfully forgotten or emotions I had locked away. For the past 27 years I had focused on raising children, being married and fundamentally placing my needs aside. How was I going to handle this journey home?

Now that it is time to leave Kerkiecoondah, I know that I have had four precious days.

A reminder of how much bigger things are from a child's perspective. How critical people in place are; that place and things are but the shell for filling in the intangibles of love, happiness and sorrow. The bungalow and huge garden

that I remembered had different proportions now. The brilliant orange of marigolds, red of cannas and bright pink of bougenvelliea hedges weren't there. The
dogs weren't racing down the driveway to greet me and neither were my smiling parents in the carport looking excited to see me. But on this trip there
was an intensity of experiencing flashes of everything that had happened here
but now in four days. As if a dry, shrink-wrapped sponge has just been opened
and dropped into water, quickly expanding and becoming full again, soaking in
every moment. I had managed to hold myself together. This is my last evening
on the Estate and Ashok's instructions are helping me realize that tomorrow
morning we are leaving for Hampi.

The 280 kilometers from the Estate to Hampi, a UNESCO World Heritage
site, would take about six hours to cover. None of us had driven to Hampi
before and we are taking this journey because I asked if they would join me.
Neither Ashok nor Meenu had been there but agreed that they both had heard
much about the place from friends and reading about this important historic site
and saw this as an opportunity to visit there. It will be a detour for Ashok and
Meenu who would normally have returned directly to Bangalore from the Estate
but they could take a few days off work. We don't have a GPS. We are doing this
based on a route mapped by Google Maps and consultations with Gautham, the
Tea Factory Manager, who had been up there once many years ago. He couldn't
remember too much about the journey other than it was hot and the first thing
they did when they arrived was get out of the car and dip their feet in the cool
waters of the lake. The lake? We know there is a river there, the Cauvery, but
a lake? Gautham printed out these directions for us to follow:

Estate to Balehonnur – N. R. Pura – Shimoga –
Hagaribommanahalli – Hospet to Hampi
(Approximate 280 to 300 K.M.)

This morning of our departure, the sun rose from behind the hills pushing past
monsoon clouds, which had dominated for weeks, reminding us that the rains
will give way to sun. The valleys are still shrouded in early morning mist and
the soft light of dawn brushes the white-washed walls of the labourers' houses

and glistens off the aluminum siding of the tea factory. This is just as I remembered it to be. An acknowledgment that I must treasure the past but it is time to let go and create my own memories of this special place. This is probably the last time I will be here. For the first twenty years of my life this was my home — where my parents lived. I have known Ashok since I was in my late teens and Meenu since she married him. Our families were close and I enjoy a sense of safety, of refuge being with them again.

"Are the sandwiches in the car? What about the water? Do you have your BlackBerry," Ashok asks me? "Where's Meenu?"

He is driving today, ready and eager to go. All in the car, we wave goodbye to Ganga, the housekeeper at the bungalow and head off down to the village at the base of the Estate and onto the main road. We pass the tea factory traffic circle and I gaze out across the acres of tea bushes, which look like hills covered in smooth carpets of green, as the car meanders down to the main gate. Ashok stops here for a few minutes to talk with the gatekeeper. I feel my eyes watering. As I blink the dam bursts and I quietly smudge the tears away with my sleeve. The car pulls through the gate, the gatekeeper closes it behind us.

With the printed Google map in hand, I am the designated navigator for the journey. "Why are you turning 'right'?" I ask "We were going to Shimoga which should be left?

"One of the visitors to the factory yesterday said that we should not take that route to Shimoga as the road is about 60 kilometers longer," Ashok replies.

Traffic is sparse so we keep an average speed of 40 km an hour; the road winds down through the jungle and coffee plantations, dark and dripping with monsoon rains. As we come down from the hills, the road takes us through the Bhadra Wildlife Sanctuary. The absence of conversation in the early morning is broken by tunes from the iPod. "Do you remember, the 21st night of September"...ba de ya, never was a cloudy day, ba de ya de ya.... Occasionally the music is interrupted by Ashok slowing down to ask for directions. Sitting in the front seat, I roll down the window and Ashok asks for directions in Kannada:

"Swami, is this the road to Haripanahali?" The confusion is evident on the listener's face who can't see the driver but this white woman asking directions in Kannada, in a man's voice? We are taking B roads all day, some potholed like a lunarscape making it impossible to drive more than 5 km an hour. Picking up the pace to 50 km an hour is rare, then slowing down again while the shepherd boy eases his goats off the centre of the road so that the bus, truck, motorbike and us can pass. As we drive through the countryside we breakfast on omelet sandwiches, sprinkled with green chilies made by Ganga. After sandwiches, the Eagles — "One of these nights" bounces around the car until a business call received on Bluetooth comes through the speakers, interrupting the sing a along. It's Rohan, Ashok and Meenu's son, from head office calling to discuss the tea prices he is negotiating with a buyer.

For miles there is no sign of life, then just as Ashok slowed to navigate another series of potholes, Meenu frantically pointed to the left side of the road.

"Look, look," she says. Yes, there are four elephants emerging from the jungle and about to cross the road — three females and a calf. Ashok hits the breaks and reverses slowly to allow them space to cross peacefully. U2 — Beautiful Day — is playing — yes it is a beau-ti-ful day, don't let it get away. Rohan has good taste in music. Our road crosses NH4 in Harihar, time to check directions.

"Yes, straightu, straightu" comes the reply with requisite head shaking. After a while you wonder if indeed it is straight or perhaps not? We need a pit stop — for petrol and bathroom. New petrol bunks are now required to build washrooms on site so we drive on looking for one of these new petrol bunks. Almost like a mirage, there on the left was a brand new Bharath Petroleum: Autofuels and Lubricants and the universal sign for washrooms. As we pull in we soon realize construction isn't quite complete — no relief here. We continue on through town and find another petrol bunk but no washroom. With one need met we continue to look for a solution to the other. There are no Rest Centers on the highways and public washrooms are rare and not necessarily ones you want to experience. Meenu is almost incapable of talking with her need to go and Ashok points out:

"The only choice now is the great outdoors." So we drive out of town, the visible population reduces significantly. It seems too that the vegetation has changed from the dense jungles to flat open plains with occasional rows of sisal, which looks like a large palm at shrub level. The plant when cut and dried is used to make hessian, the hessian used in sacks before plastic was introduced. There are big, old banyan trees along the road but these have tall naked trunks as goats have eaten all the low hanging leaves, leaving a healthy crown to provide cool shade. As Meenu is scouting the horizon for the ultimate stop, it seems that the traffic has picked up. A vehicle is passing about every four minutes. Finally Ashok pulls over: "We'll stop here, pick your tree!"

"But look at the cars coming and over there in the field there are people working" protests Meenu. By now Ashok has crossed the road to find his tree of choice. Meenu heads off and I watch the car and shout if anyone heads in Meenu's direction.

Hrapanahalli – Just try saying this word – Hra-pan-a-halli – you have to roll your tongue around for the 'r' and the rest flows. Here we stop a middle aged man for directions then head north to NH 63, Hospet and the Tungabhadra Reservoir. This must be the lake the tea factory Manager was talking about. It is much drier and hotter in this part of the countryside. We are definitely getting closer to our destination. Meenu starts to share some of the historical highlights about Hampi. I never knew she was such a local historian.

"Hampi used to be the seat of the Vijayanagara kingdom. About 700 years ago it was South India's cultural center, precious stones, diamonds, rubies, emeralds and other gems all over. It has an olympic-sized swimming pool for everyone to use. It is a remarkable place. Hindus come here on pilgrimage and more adventurous Westerners interested in history and a glimpse into a society, which is believed to be the foundations of the Ramayana. Being a bit off the regular tourist routes so you have to really want to come here. It used to be just the Hippies but now tourists from everywhere come here," says Meenu.

Getting here from Bangalore is quite a journey by train or bus or even tourist bus, unless you have friends who can drive you or hire a taxi. When you see where the remains of the kingdom are located, it makes you wonder why this particular place was chosen to be the capital of this ancient society. It is remote, hard to reach, seemingly rocky barren land that would be hard to grow crops. The Tungabhadra River being the one benefit.

"The site is so huge you can't just walk around it — so we'll take an Auto. When were you last in an Auto Charlie? We'll all squeeze into one so don't eat too much for breakfast" laughs Ashok. "That's also why we are staying two nights because there is no way we can see everything in one day. We can start this afternoon after we've checked in at the hotel."

"You know it was cousin Samir who got me interested in local history and I just got the bug," said Meenu.

"Yes I remember Samir talking about Hampi. He must have visited with friends years ago. It was about 10 year between when I last saw him and when he died. In fact I think the last time was when we met in Berkeley for lunch one day. I can't believe he passed away," I say with difficulty in saying those words 'I can't believe he passed away'. We've talked about Samir since he died but it doesn't get any easier.

"Look there's the sign for Hampi UNESCO World Heritage Site. We have arrived in the town but I have no idea where the hotel is from here," said Ashok as he drives across the railway tracks, weaving past large colourful trucks. Hospet is a major intersection for freight railway lines in the area so the truck density increases. It is also the town nearest to Hampi and we are staying at the Royal Orchid Hotel. We come to a halt along with a melee of other vehicles trying to navigate the approach to the traffic circle. Ashok asks the driver in the Land Rover next to us:

"Which way to the Royal Orchid Hotel?"

"Go up to the round about, turn right then left at the next fork, then one kilometer on you'll see it on your left. But follow me as I'm going up to the fork also."

"OK thank you," says Ashok with a wave.

Urban traffic in Hospet is much like Bangalore but many times a smaller town. We crawl to the roundabout where everything comes to a halt again. Bullock cart on one side of us, trucks, cars, pedestrian carts, all momentarily at a stop. With gradual inching in the direction you want to go, the gridlock slowly unfolds as momentum accelerates and within about 7 minutes all vehicles spiral out to their chosen direction; us off down the street to the fork in the road. The

Land Rover driver has sped ahead but pulled over and is pointing in the direction we need to take, then waves and is gone. Within minutes we arrive at the hotel. A peculiar oasis of high rise, polished granite floors, a large cool lobby with staff to welcome you after what would be a long and tiring journey for any traveller. Being slightly off-season the hotel has fewer guests than usual so the elevators are switched off to conserve electricity and all guests are being housed in the garden level rooms.

This evening we eat dinner on the lawn. The evening screening of a popular Hindi movie is on the outdoor movie screen and being half watched by people enjoying their sundowners with an occasional glance at the screen. Just as Meenu is ordering her chicken biryani a blast of a song cut through everything. People are gathering for evening prayer at the temple across the street and the accompanying music and song are far louder than anything imaginable. Even the movie is drowned out. We can't hear ourselves speak and the remainder of the ordering is done by pointing at the menu. The waiter assures us, with many gesticulations, that this will die down shortly.

The next day, the three of us bounce around in the auto rickshaw as the driver scoots us to the various key sites in Hampi. We walk around the ruins, to the elephant stables, through the Queen's Bath, into temples, up granite monoliths, past the kissing rocks and down to the river for a rest. We eat thali in the riverside restaurant and drink chai. Seeing the landscape you wonder why Hampi was the centre of a kingdom with such riches. Miles of stony ground, dotted with granite monoliths and the great Tungabhadra river. In the 21 century, Bangalore is the 'kingdom' of the south. Once the 'Garden City of India' with a more laid-back demeanor is now an international tech hub bursting with the energy of anticipation of what each individual can become. Urban growth so vast and fast that a new international airport was built so that travellers can bypass Mumbai or Delhi and go directly to Bangalore from Frankfurt, London and other major cities.

It is exciting to explore this ancient city of Hampi, to learn about the history of an area, which has so strongly impacted the lives of generations of my family, yet one I had never visited before. I know I have left the tea and coffee plantations behind me and because of that carry the weight of melancholy. But I am buoyed by the future, the warmth of friends, and this journey that binds us. I'm not sure if I have finally accepted that the past is gone; I still don't understand what happened with Samir. I hope he died feeling happy, feeling loved. But this journey has strengthened the friendship with Ashok and Meenu to lead me forward. For now, it is the gift of friendship I treasure.

Hampi

Understanding

AUGUST 2012

THE ROARING FLAMES AND CRACKLING wood of the tea factory furnace hypnotize me. The intensity of the heat forces me to step back but I remain entranced and for a few moments as my mind drifts back to those times when I shadowed my father on his rounds through the tea factory. I understand now that it was the foundation of our relationship. He was focused on the business discussions with the tea factory manager and it was my responsibility to keep my fingers out of the machinery, be quiet and don't lag behind. I became an acute observer, understood body language and non-verbal cues. The silent years of teenage hood seemed to magnify the non-verbal communication between us. That's why fishing became a perfect activity for us to do together. We could enjoy the landscape, the animals, birds, the excitement in the moment of actually catching a fish but never have to say too much to each other.

JUNE 1966

The tea factory is a tall, four-story building made of aluminum and lots of glass hung together on an iron frame. These factories are never made of wood. Too much of a fire hazard, as my father well understood. One had burned down under his watch on a different estate. Tea factories are painted steel grey. They can be seen for miles, glistening in the sunlight, standing out above the sea of green tea bushes all cut to the same perfect height; this one is surrounded by the rolling hills of the Western Ghats. The tallest, largest building in the district also provided the most stunning views from the fourth floor, across smooth green hillsides of neatly planted and cut tea bushes interspersed with silver oak shade trees. On the horizon, jungle covered valleys and hills and a great blue sky. There was one more floor – the loft where all sorts of 'stuff' was stored in a very random manner – from old conveyor belts, boxes of nuts and bolts, screws, washers – you name it – the spare was there. We always started on the fourth floor where uniform and freshly harvested stems of 'two leaves and a bud', plucked by mostly women in the field, were spread out on long withering troughs. Here warm air blew along the underside to wilt the tea leaves. When the leaves were ready, the women gathered up the wilted leaves and tossed down a long chute to the ground floor, into the grinding and rolling room where men seemed to work. It was almost impossible to hear each other speak above the noise of the machinery that ground up the leaves into an unrecognizable state that released a strong smell of crushed green leaves. This was a cool room with smooth cement floors, frequently washed, always clean. From here the crushed leaves were transported by conveyer belts to the drying room which was an even noisier place, as engines turned the huge metal drums, like a clothes drier but much bigger, to remove the moisture. Once the tea was dry, this granular, brown substance emerged, more familiar to most people – tea – the most important non alcoholic beverage in the world (Kew Royal Botanical Gardens). The intense dry heat gave way to the sifting room, which was much cooler and quieter but still dry. Here the dried tea passed along a conveyor belt sifter and funneled off into wooden tea chests, lined with aluminum foil, ready to leave the factory.

The most sacred place was the tea tasting room. This space was always kept immaculately clean and almost silent, unlike the noise for the other rooms in the factory. With windows on all four sides starting as about hip height, you could see all that was going on around at the different stages and equally everyone could see in. The white ceramic Victorian sink was kept antiseptically clean. The polished granite countertop was the stage for the white china tea tasting cups and brew pots. These pots, with inverted lids, displayed the texture of the brown brewed tea leaves and were lined up along the counter behind the cups filled with tea for tasting, the glowing orange and dark brown liquid.

I watched my father use the soup spoon to sip a sample from each cup, inhaling the tea through his clenched front teeth and swooshing it around his mouth for a few seconds, eyes closed, thinking about the flavor, before spitting it out into the sink. As with wine, you never drink the tea when tasting. This was all part of the ritual, the quality control. In silence the tea factory manager waited anxiously for the pronouncement.

I could sense his apprehension.

"Very good Ramesh."

Then after a little more conversation we were off in the Jeep to see the tea nursery, where the young tea seedlings are nurtured until they are planted in the field. Then home for a cuppa. Every afternoon, after our four o'clock tea, Mum would round up the dogs - Blackie, Sandy, Moses and Spats for our constitutional family walk. The hill behind the factory was a favourite route of mine. The views across the hills and valleys were spectacular, with the tea gardens on the down slope of the hill and jungle and grasslands on the up side – the view we could see from the 4th floor. The dogs raced ahead picking up a smorgasbord of smells to chase no matter how much bigger than them, their target was. On a particularly exciting evening they would chase muntjck deer out of the jungle across the dene but most often it was hares and peacocks. On a bad evening one of the dogs yelped in pain having got too curious with a porcupine and ended up with needles stuck in its nose. Dad would have to drive them home and with some help hold them down while using a cloth rag to pull out the needles. Mum would clean the wounds and nurse them back to good health. Wild boar were another surprise for the dogs as boar are fearless and chased the dogs, right back to us. During the non-monsoon months the sunsets were always an exclamation point at the end of these evening walks, when we'd sit on a rock together for a few minutes watching the sun go down – the only noise being the exhausted dogs, seated with tongues hanging out the side of their mouth, panting from the chase and glad of a few minutes rest. They knew it was almost time to go home for their dinner and a nice relaxing evening, sleeping on the carpet in the living room, dreaming of that rabbit that got away or the boar that nearly got them.

AUGUST 2012

The fire stoker throws two more logs into the furnace then slams the iron door shut. I'm snapped out of the fire-induced daze. Here I am, Charlie, thirty years later in the same place. Not much has changed. The factory isn't as big as I remembered it to be, some of the equipment is modernized. The old aluminum-foil lined, wooden tea chests have been replaced with nylon hessian-style sacks. The faces of those working here are of a younger generation. The pungent smell of moist, crushed green leaves floods my mind with memories, I can almost hear Dad talking "Come on Charlie, keep up, I don't want to lose you in the factory". Tea tasting is still a ritual in the process.

As I stand in front of this furnace I realize that the power of the moment is the connection I'm rediscovering with my father. He was snatched from me 14 years ago, no warning, no time to say goodbye. No time for me to say thank you for this relationship you gave me with India. It seems possible now, to separate my childhood attachments to India from those I have developed on my own as an independent woman. Perhaps it is a kind of emotional suttee that allows me to throw these memories of good and bad into the fire to allow me to look forward and not linger in the past. I can finally get rid of my emotional baggage, my saamaan, and move to a new space. And I thank the gods – all of them and Ganesh in particular, the elephant faced deity with four arms, for having given me this time in South India. Ganesh is celebrated between mid August and mid September - it was always a reminder for me that summer holidays were coming to an end, school would soon begin again and I'd be back on that plane to London. Store fronts, homes and parks came alive with every size statue of large pink elephants with human limbs, adorned in other bright colours as everyone seemed to prepare for this festival. A sense of happiness in the air.

As I understand all this I'm ready to let the lines blur again, let one memory melt into the other like the rich reds of a Mysore sunset. I'll keep that warmth wrapped around me as I prepare for the impending melancholy of another winter in Vancouver. On those dreary days, the best antidote is a cup of tea.

Ganesh

GLOSSARY

Amma	Mother
Appa	Father
Aya	Nanny
Bangalore	State capital of Karnataka. Now known as Bengaluru.
Bangalore Club	A Social club where coffee & tea planters stayed when visiting the city.
Belur and Halebide	16 kilometers apart, these temples were the capital of the Hoysala Empire in the 12th century.
Brinjal	Eggplant, aubergine
Brahmin	An individual born into that cast, a priest, an educator, vegetarian
Cutthie	Small curved machete
Dosa	Thick, crispy pancake made of rice and black lentil flour, filled with spiced boiled potatoes & cauliflower, served with samba & coconut/mint chutney.
Dhurrie	Cotton weave rug or blanket to sit on, on the ground
Ganesh	Hindu Elephant Deity – Lord of Success
Ice Factory	Place where you buy huge blocks of ice to transport goods that need to be chilled
Kannada	Language of Karnataka State (formerly Mysore State)
Kashmiri shawl	A luxurious woolen shawl with an intricate embroidered pattern
Kedgeree	A rice dish using saffron to colour the rice, includes sardines, hard boiled eggs, crispy fried onions and cashew nuts.
Kerkiecoondah	Tea and coffee plantation/estate in Chikmagalur District
Mahout	Elephant driver/jockey
Masala	Mixture of spices
Mehndi	Henna paste squeezed through an icing cone to draw intricate designs on the back of your hand or feet, usually during wedding celebrations.

Monsoon	Refers to the two main rainy seasons in India – the south-west and the northeast monsoons. Monsoons also affect other parts of Southeast Asia and Africa.
Mysore	Formerly the Capital of Mysore State, during the time of the Maharajas. Now known as Mysuru.
Namaste	Greeting – hello or farewell
Nimbu	Lime
Nimbu pani	Lime juice with water, (bitter without sugar, great with gin)
Puja	Indian prayer ceremony
Saamaan	Baggage, luggage of the physical kind (in this context used as 'emotional baggage'
Salaam	Salute of acknowledgement often followed by a greeting.
Samba	Lentil based soup with chopped vegetables, served with dosa.
Seringapatam	Now known as Srirangapatna
Sravanabelagola	Jain temple complex to Gomateshwara Bhagwaan Bahubali
Syce	Groom, stable hand

BIBLIOGRAPHY

The Practice
Almost four hundred years of legal practice in a Welsh county town
By Quentin Dodd
Published in 2003 by Bridge Books

Hampi
By D. Devakunjari Revised by B. Narasimhaiah
Published by Archeological Survey of India
New Delhi 2007

The sword of Tipu Sultan
Bhagwan S. Gidwani
Allied Publishers Private Limited 1978

Tea

About the Author

Charlotte Lawson was born in India and spent her childhood and early adulthood shuttling between England and India. Her time in India left her very familiar with the places of Karnataka and many friendships.

Lawson's family had a long history in India, and she explored temples and ruins with a personal interest. She combined her love of adventure and horses while working on a thoroughbred farm in Hassan. Visits to Karnataka over the past five years have given her opportunity to observe the changes—both subtle and dramatic—and understand her connection to India.

A mother of two adult children, Lawson can be found cycle touring and planning her next trip to India when she is not working. She holds a BA in geography, an MA in education and is a graduate of The Writer's Studio, Simon Fraser University's creative writing program. She now lives in Vancouver, Canada.

CPSIA information can be obtained at www.ICGtesting.com
Printed in the USA
LVOW06s1209061215

465426LV00035B/87/P

9 781517 503024